To A Dancing God

Sam Keen

To a
Dancing
God

HARPER & ROW, PUBLISHERS
NEW YORK, EVANSTON, AND LONDON

LIBRARY OF CONGRESS CATALOG CARD NUMBER: 79-109061

Contents

For my mother Ruth McMurray Keen
Who taught me by example
to search out my own truth
and nurtured in me
a strong and tender trust
which has survived
the death of many beliefs

To A Dancing God

Introduction

Once upon a time there was an unchanging God who was king over an orderly world in which change occurred so benevolently it was called progress. There was a place and a time for everything. Six days for work and one for being told the meaning of work. And certain things were not done on Sunday. There were authorities too. The minister and priest spoke without hesitation of God and his requirements. Dad and Mother told us what good boys and girls did (or mostly didn't do). The newspaper told it like it was. Uncle Sam could be trusted to make the world safe for democracy. And filling in all the cracks between constituted authorities were reason and common sense.

Then something happened. Some say God died. This much we know: everything that was nailed down suddenly came loose. Chaos was king and the moral world looked like a furniture store after a hurricane. Everywhere the credentials of the authorities were challenged and great impostors were discovered in high circles. The consensus about morals disintegrated in pluralism. The credibility of revelation, and therefore the whole massive structure of organized religion, was gradually eroded away by empirical and pragmatic habits of thought. Uncle Sam lost all claim to the unquestioned allegiance of his citizens by his immoral conduct in Vietnam and his insane flirtation with ABM's and defense strategies based upon the calculation of mega-death capacity. The authority of reason also became tarnished as it became clear that the university, no less than any other institution, shaped its conclusions to satisfy its desires. And, alas, it even began to appear that boys and girls who refrained from doing what Dad and Mother had forbidden might be rewarded more by neurosis than beatitude.

So what is there left to trust? Perhaps even this story about the death of the authorities is false. There is no way to tell for certain because there are no authorities to tell us. When the gods speak with conflicting voices, or are silent, the men must decide. If authority has collapsed where is the individual to discover the principles of a style of life which is authentic? Indeed, by what criteria is he to decide what an "authentic" life-style is?

It is at this point of crisis and quest that these essays begin.

I cannot say for certain whether the once-upon-a-time story I have told about the life and death of the authorities is true. Perhaps I am attributing to the historical process what is merely an individual experience. I do know that I have undergone a process of disillusionment with the authorities I was taught to trust and I have found it necessary to search for the foundations of my identity and dignity in the intimate, sensuous, idiosyncratic elements of my own experience. I have had to discover the principles without which I could not be. I share my reflections because I am convinced that my story is not atypical.

I, Sam Keen, wrote this book. The voice that speaks to you in these essays is mine. It is not the voice of Philosophy, or Theology, or Modern Man. What I offer is a series of personal reflections upon issues, problems, and crises with which I have had to wrestle. The conclusions I have reached are not inescapable. Both my doubts and my certainties may be too intimately connected to unique elements in my autobiography to be typical of that nebulous creature called "modern man." When I speak with assurance it is because I have discovered some elements of a style of life that are satisfying for me. However, the affirmations I make have no authority unless you choose to add your voice to mine. This is how it is with me. I cannot say how it is with you. Nevertheless I would invite you to replace the "I" of these essays with "we" when you find yourself in agreement.

It takes considerable discipline to say "I" rather than to appeal to the authority of the anonymous "one," or the plural "we," or the mythical "modern man," or the venerable "Christian tradition," or the popular "common sense." And to refrain from excessive footnoting requires more than a little courage for one trained in the academy. In writing these essays I have had a growing need to write in the first-person singular, to refrain from hiding behind stylistic devices which are designed to give the reader the impression that an authority or an oracle rather than a person is speaking. My discipline and my courage have often failed. To write as a single person, to take responsibility for all the statements I make, requires greater vulnerability (that is humility) and self-assurance than I possess. However, my failure is an important part of the *process* which these essays exemplify and, therefore, I have not rewritten the earlier essays to eliminate the sentences and paragraphs that seem to have been produced by an anonymous and discarnate author.

Some words about the terrain covered by this book may be helpful. The questions which have concerned me most consistently are concentrated in an area where theology, philosophy, psychology and political thought overlap. I can designate this area most clearly by an analogy.

There is a species of mushroom, *Marasmius oreades,* which behaves in a fashion very satisfactory to geometers. It propagates itself in circles. On the green turf, in an open pasture land, it will enclose a grassy space with a ring of yellow buds . . . . The visible order of these mushrooms is so tidy and engaging that even Plato might have been induced to look a second time at this womb-of-becoming. They are in fact, as the curious have come to know, the

organs of a single spawn, all connected with that center by subterranean filaments, by the mycelium, as botanists call it, so that
their center is not in fact ideal, but material enough, simply, like
the loves of geometers, not visible on the surface. A little digging
will discover it, nor does it deserve less to be celebrated that its
geometry is realized, like yours and mine, out of clay. It is
nevertheless, that mycelium, the tangible emblem of what in
reflection men call a principle, that connection which, being
known, gives understanding, and which, being buried, requires
in the interest of understanding, to be dug up.*

These essays are an exploration of the mycelium. They are
philosophical in the classical sense because they seek to go
beneath the surface to expose the foundations or principles
which support, unify, clarify, dignify, beautify, and sanctify
human life. Their autobiographical bias marks them as
belonging to that species of philosophy which has lately been
called existentialism.

It would not be unfair also to consider this a series of
investigations of the possibility of doing theology after "the
death of God." I confess I see little difference between philosophy and theology (properly done). When theology abandons
the claim to revelation and ceases to speak with institutional
authority it becomes a species of philosophy; and when
philosophy uncovers principles or structures which are the
preconditions of human wholeness it discovers the sacred. A
phenomenological approach shows that the sacred is what
founds, grounds, and sustains. Therefore a philosophy which
discovers the mycelium is also a subterranean theology. (Only
a subterranean theology is radical and earthy enough to support
the underground church.) Thus if this book be theology it is
concerned with the proximate rather than the remote, the native
rather than the imported, the quotidian rather than the ex-

* John F. A. Taylor, "Politics and the Human Covenant," *Centennial Review*
71, No. 1 (1962), p. 1.

traordinary, the natural rather than the occult, the humanistic rather than the ecclesiastical, the sacred rather than God.

The dancing god to whom the title of this book refers is neither Apollo nor Dionysus. Indeed, he is nameless and, perhaps, must remain so. My (our?) only assurance is that he inhabits me (us?) as often in discipline as in spontaneity, as much in decision as in ecstasy, as frequently in promises as in immediacy. As always, the sacred shatters all the categories we necessarily use to understand the sacred. So the dance continues. That is life. And for it I wish to offer these libations.

Finally, I would like to express my gratitude to the American Association of Theological Schools, Louisville Presbyterian Seminary, Western Behavioral Sciences Institute and Center for Studies of the Person for grants, fellowships, and other forms of support, visible and invisible, which allowed me to write this book.

One | *Exile and Homecoming*

How may I live gracefully in time? In my times?

The clock is ticking the minutes away. My minutes. Each tick synchronizes with a heartbeat. Now inside and out the measured movement of time carries me forward toward, toward, toward, toward (my mind stutters to avoid the end of the sentence, to avoid the end, to avoid the sentence). My attention turns from the anxious uncertainties and the final certainty of the future, in search of a more secure harbor. I pass quickly through the turbulent inlet of the present and work my way into the quiet upstream waters of the past, further and further until I come to rest on a summer day when I was eight. I am driving up into the mountains with my family. It won't be long until we reach Apple Buchanan's house. We come down the final hill. There is the swing that goes high out over the valley. We rush to see who will get the first turn. Dad climbs up the hill pulling the cable until he gets to the launching platform. Here I go! Out over the valley into orbit (connected to earth only by the hickory stick I am sitting on and the steel swing cable) and back over the stream and the cow pasture and the smell of apples and pine smoke. Out and back, out and back. The pendulum dies slowly and I come to rest in the dust at the bottom of the swing. "Daddy, I want to swing again, take me back up the hill." Dad, Dad, Dad—dead. Tick, tick tick and then the ticker stops. The panic begins to squeeze my breath out. I have to get out of here! Out of the past. There is no harbor in memory safe from death; there is dis-ease in the future and in the past. I have only one hope. I coerce myself into the here and now, into the sounds (jet roar, sea pound, heartbeat) and the sensations of the moment (warm sun, cool skin, salt air, sticky typewriter keys). I hone my attention well, hoping it will cut to the heart of significance. I concentrate. I pass through many metamorphoses; I become— a white thumbtack on a red board, a dog's tail wagging against a blue sky, an itch between the toes, a sign saying PRIVATE PROPERTY. I pass from interest to interest, but am not satisfied. Still dis-eased, twisting, turning, running forward and backward in my time. A bone out of socket. A wanderer in exile.

I | Exile—A Study in Nostalgia

Nostalgia is the symptom of exile, the mark of dis-eased time. An exile is a sojourner in the present, consumed with longing for a homeland which lies in the past or the future. Fulfillment is always contingent upon return to the mythical golden age of "once upon a time" or residence in the alabaster

city of tomorrow. Exile is longing for what was or will be;
living in memory or anticipation; straining for validation (the
Good Housekeeping seal of approval).

Nostalgia speaks many languages and assumes many dis-
guises. Old-timers remember the good old days when there
were wooden ships and iron men, free enterprise and nickel
beer. Religious folk remember Eden, anticipate the New
Jerusalem, treasure splinters of the True Cross and ankle bones
of men who walked in the sacred time of the Lord. Sophisticated suburbanites in functional homes collect old medicine
bottles, Model A Fords, reproductions of authentic early American furniture, convert trivia into vintage. ("Do you remember
the unsurpassed performance of Humphrey Bogart in the
Maltese Falcon?") Or the longing may be directed toward
the future: "When I get to heaven I'm going to put on my
shoes . . . ." "When I get the mortgage paid off I'm going to
get in my car and . . . ." "When I lose my anxiety about sex,
I'm going to . . . ." Then is when I'll be happy, secure, satisfied.
Just as soon as I have finished this book . . . . In the sweet by-
and-by when we get to that beautiful shore. Where *"it* is at"
is always somewhere else: Long ago and far away, or just
around the corner in the Garden of Eden or the classless society.

A man wanders in exile until he has discovered the "once
upon a time" and the "someday" which give shape to his
personal longing and demythologizes the public or private
myths by which he has lived. My own wandering in the desert
began in the promised land of Israel.

Memories and Expectations of
a Pseudo-Israelite

It was in Tennessee that I first learned about the history of
my native land, in partition-divided Sunday school rooms
covered with pictures and maps of the Holy Land. Before I
was six I had walked through Judea, Galilee, Capernaum,

Bethlehem, Jerusalem, sharing a dusty road with Jesus and the disciples, finding at day's end the comfort of a footbath, bread and olives in a humble home. And what a rich time and place it was to which I belonged! Over these hills and desert places my forebears—Abraham, Isaac, David, and Solomon—had roamed, killing the enemies of the Lord and establishing a kingdom for the children of promise. From papier-mâché models I learned the architecture of the Holy Land, and from bathrobe dramas its way of dress (and at recess there was milk and graham crackers). I learned of Deborah's heroism (but not of Molly Pitcher's) and of the judges and kings the Lord raised to lead and chastise his people (but not of the judges of Blount County who helped to keep whiskey illegal and bootlegging profitable). I knew the topography of Judea before I could locate the Cumberland Plateau, as I knew the road from Damascus to Jerusalem before I could find my way from Maryville to Knoxville.

Sitting astride the Holy Land was the figure of Jesus, my model, my savior, my judge, and my Lord. Jesus loved me, this I knew. I had a friend in Jesus who could walk with me in Tennessee and give me guidance, succor, and assurance. Although I sang "It may not be on a mountain top or over a stormy sea, it may not be on the battle front, my Lord will have need of me," I had every good hope that I would be permitted the privilege of manning a post where the battle with the enemies of the righteous raged strong. I longed to be counted with the heroes and saints. I prepared for the place Jesus would assign me in history by arming myself with the Word of Truth (The Bible—King James Version—Schofield notes) and by keeping in frequent contact with headquarters by way of prayer. There was not often doubt in my mind about what Jesus required, although there was frequent resistance when I suspected that the enemies I was called upon to love and convert to the faith were none other than the dreaded Long boys whose depravity was obvious (they smoked real cigarettes filched from their father's store while the rest of us were limited to rabbit tobacco and corn silk). I was sometimes fearful that the final test of discipleship might confront me—the choice between my parents and the Lord. Although the evidence suggested they were among the most loyal disciples of Christ, I knew that someday a decisive moment would come when I would have to demonstrate my total commitment in some mysterious and unnatural way. "Once to every man and nation comes the moment to decide . . ." For the time being, Jesus required only gentleness and abstinence from the obvious sins (smoking, lying, stealing, swearing, going to the movies, questioning orthodox theology, sex, and a frivolous enjoyment of the world). With all seriousness and commitment I prepared for the hard task of living as a heavenly exile in the midst of a sinful world. A wayfaring stranger traveling through this world of woe must be armed against the seductions of this age. There is always the danger that cheerfulness might break in and dispel the serious truth that all men are sinners whose only hope is in casting themselves on the mercy of Jesus Christ.

Of course I constantly fell short of the ideal of Jesus, repented, and renewed my resolve to follow in the footsteps of the Master. Although I knew the sanctity required of me was not within range of my will power, there was the ever-present possibility that the kingdom of God would arrive momentarily and purge me of my unholiness. In the small towns of Alabama, Florida, and Tennessee in which I lived it was common knowledge among the righteous that we were living in the Last Days before the end of the world. There was widespread disagreement about the details of the coming kingdom. Some considered Mussolini to be the beast with 666 upon his forehead who, according to the book of Revelation, would usher in the kingdom of evil which was to arrive shortly before the triumph of the saints. Some accorded this honor to Hitler. Not a few stanch Republicans were certain that F.D.R. was the Antichrist. In my childish mind the situation was vastly confused because

666 was also the trade name of a widely advertised headache remedy. Each rival candidate for the Antichrist had loyal followers who could prove their claimant's case with cryptic quotes from Daniel, Revelation, or Mark 13. I seem to recall that once in a fit of anger I announced that my brother was the "abomination of desolation" (as indeed he could be). There was lively controversy whether Jesus was to establish his dominion immediately or only after defeating the Antichrist and overthrowing his one-thousand-year kingdom. To the pagan or worldly-wise this may seem an academic issue. But to those who were awaiting the immediate conclusion of history it was of some concern whether they were to be ushered into the premillennial reign of the Antichrist or the kingdom of God.

Whatever minor differences in interpretation clouded the picture, the outline was clear. The present age was the decadent conclusion of history. Evil had progressed in its dominion over history to the point where God was forced to intervene. Christians were exiles and pilgrims in this evil age of creeping socialism, modernism, loose morals, and increasing leisure. Salvation belonged only to those who were willing to forsake the ways of the world and live for the coming kingdom. It was strongly implied that the only authentic vocation for the born-again Christian was preaching the gospel to the pagans and bringing the saving knowledge of Jesus Christ to the world. The future belonged to those who planned for it, who turned their present into a quest for sanctity. Anything less than total allegiance to Jesus was betrayal. The authentic life combined disdain and suspicion of the present age with nostalgia for the Holy Land and longing for the kingdom which was to come.

As I approached puberty my nostalgia for ancient Israel and for the New Jerusalem came into conflict with a dark longing that was born in dreams of ecstasy. The voice of the body called me back into the present. The contest between Jesus who was Lord of the past and the future and the life-sap that rises in

the green body of adolescence proved unequal. My loyalties
split. Even as my spirit hoped for the triumph of holiness, my
body prayed that the kingdom would not arrive and find me still
a virgin. It was impossible to rejoice in the promises that "in
Christ there would be neither male nor female" and that in the
kingdom of God there would be no marriage when I had not
yet enjoyed the mystery of sex.

It was some time after my body began to demand satisfactions more immediate than those promised by the kingdom of
God that my mind also joined the rebellion. With rising
anxiety I discovered that the history which I had taken as the
basis of my identity was fallible. Historical and textual criticism
of the Bible yielded a high degree of probability that many of
the old, old stories were only that. The evidence suggested that
many of the "mighty acts of God" did not happen and that the
whole schema of promise and fulfillment which was the heart
of the Christian idea of history was superimposed by the biblical authors *ex post facto*. I learned of messiahs before and after
Jesus who died as martyrs; and of the long process of political
and ecclesiastical infighting which only gradually created the
orthodoxy I had believed to be inseparable from the events.
And I learned of gnostic redeemers who came to earth (or almost to earth) and died and rose again. As the conclusion became inevitable—my history as an Israelite had been constructed
by men and not by God—my mind joined with my body in demanding that I leave Israel and come home to America.

The crisis came in the early hours of a February morning
within view of the Harvard Yard. The armies of the Lord
faced the army of Truth. On the one side was all that I had
believed about heaven and earth and my dazzling aspirations
toward purity, sanctity, and obedience to a known God. On the
other side a restlessness in the loins, a handful of facts that
would not be denied, and a wilderness which hinted of both
terror and adventure. The issue was so drawn for me, that the
choice was between remaining a Christian or becoming honest.

The armies defending the Holy Land fought to the last before yielding. Exhausted, I slept. I awoke at noon in Cambridge, Mass., U.S.A., and after coffee and rolls, began to create the world.

An Existentialist Interlude— Projecting the Future and Discovering the Past

From religious history and eschatology I turned to existentialism and the effort to project my own future and reconstruct my own past.

In the early 1950's, when I began to look to philosophy for the wholeness I had not found in religion, it was existentialism that first caught my attention. The popular press was then fond of printing pictures of beautiful, haunted girls and bearded men and giving accounts of their wild actions. Some, it was hinted, lived like the lilies of the field (or the animals of the jungle) with complete sexual abandon, taking no thought for the morrow. In each generation the media find it necessary to create an image of a group that embodies the ideals of spontaneity, anarchism, and freedom from all respectable repressions.

With a faith born of long dependence upon the Book I turned to libraries and classrooms to find the path to the kingdom of now. No sooner was I within the doors of the academy than I discovered an existentialism which was the polar opposite of the one which had first attracted me. From Kierkegaard, Heidegger, Camus, and Sartre I learned to suspect hope, love, and other tenderminded attitudes and to hold anxiety and anguish in high regard. As I struggled to earn the honorific "modern man" I plunged deep into nihilism and rose again with stoic courage to construct from my interior resources an abode in a dark and careless world.

Sartre provided me the most useful tools for building a new identity, a new eschatology. Where Christianity had taught me that the future would come as a gift bringing completeness and satisfaction, Sartre insisted that I could have no authentic present without assuming the awful responsibility of creating a project to give my life meaning. To be is to become. All human dignity rests upon deciding upon some project and engaging in the action appropriate to the end chosen. The authentic man is teleologically oriented; his end justifies his means; his chosen future redeems his present from emptiness and nausea. It was up to me to give my life dignity, meaning, and value by resolving and achieving.

My first decision was to marry a pagan. I had been dating Heather while still a spiritual resident of Israel. However, at the time it was clear to me she would not make a suitable wife. Wise believers do not yoke themselves to unbelievers, no matter how attractive. Attending to the serious business of the kingdom of God requires a total commitment. As a private citizen of the contemporary world, however, I chose to yield to the promise of a satisfying present and future. I became loyal to my desires rather than obedient to my duties, and was rewarded with the first taste of graceful freedom.

Although I did not realize it at the time, I began to invest heavily in a dream, a project, a future which was designed to justify my existence. In my ignorance I exchanged the blueprints of the kingdom of God for another kingdom of the future but retained the old life style—postponing satisfaction, living expectantly toward some future event which would make me a complete human being. My nostalgia was for that time when I would complete my Ph.D. and become a professor. When I achieved that goal I had every confidence the magic would descend upon me—tightness would give way to looseness, the void would become a plenum, anguish would be replaced by satisfaction.

Trusting in such promises I endured the desert of graduate education. I accepted exile from the present as the price of purchasing a future that would give dignity and density to my existence. I turned aside from the task of cultivating the native soil of my experience and became a sharecropper in intellectual fields of absentee owners. I listened to the wisdom of Socrates and Aristotle, Kant and Hegel, Tillich and Marcel. Yet I was rude to Sam Keen. I ignored his boredom, I repressed his fantasies, I resented his impatience with intellectual games, I silenced the voice of his senses that called out for delight, I turned off the inner music that set his ideas and his body dancing. I asked him to submit to the discipline of language requirements, area requirements, papers, reports, projects, exams, lectures, seminars, in order that he might earn the credentials for creative thinking. I promised him that once the criteria had been met, the authorities satisfied, the degree achieved, he might have the privilege of stating a proposition or two of his own (hopefully, properly footnoted, to show the historical and contemporary precedents and similarities).

One advantage of religious eschatology is that the kingdom does not come and thus the life-style of expectancy need not be shattered. Ph.D's, however, are sometimes completed. There is a tradition at Princeton that it does not rain on graduation day. Thus it was a fitting symbolic conclusion of my graduate education (which valued tradition more than immediate reality) that my degree should be awarded in a substantial downpour in an outdoor ceremony. U Thant, the invited dignitary, looked unperturbed through it all. Raindrops gathered at the end of the tassel on my mortarboard. And the president of Princeton talked about what we would do *if* it should rain.

Now that the future had arrived I set about to enjoy it. After thirty years of preparation I had graduated into responsible life. The first few times someone referred to me as DR. Keen an electrical shock ran through my spine. There was also the brief satisfaction of designing and giving a series of courses and learning how to lecture and conduct seminars with professional skill. But the enjoyment began to dwindle. The kingdom of God became a drag: papers to grade, committees, faculty

meetings and endless talk, talk, talk, and review books accumu-
lating on my shelves. The future for which I had sacrificed
arrived, but the promised satisfaction did not.

With a flurry of energy I ran to avoid the voices heralding
the arrival of emptiness, I returned to my existentialist mentors
—to polish up my resolve and make new projects. I decided that
I would make new decisions. I would create a career for myself,
learn how to play the games philosophers play, give lectures
and write books. In the end, perhaps, I might look back on what
I had accomplished and not be dissatisfied.

It didn't work. My resolve was short of breath; my will easily
became unglued from its object; my attention lagged. Disappointment, once tasted, remains in the system like sour garlic.
I had twice sought nourishment from dreams yet I was still
filled with longing. I was still in exile.

What followed is difficult to describe with accuracy because
its essence was confusion. It was as if my interior space had
been hollowed out and boredom, anxiety, despair, impotence,
erratic willfulness, and shameful self-consciousness were
dumped in and agitated like clothes in a washer. These demons
whirled around my inner emptiness, their harsh screams rever-
berating and blending into painful cacophony in the vacuum.
I was possessed by vertigo. No way to stop the swirl. No solid
ground. No place to rest. No power to discover or cling to what
was satisfying.

Only once the vertigo disappeared. *The* phone call came.
My father was dying. Before I reached Arizona the unthinkable
tyranny of death had established its rule over all the worlds I
would ever know. The gods were dead and I was alone in the
sacred silence that follows the collapse of the last great illusion
of childhood—the illusion that death has no dominion over The
Father (and therefore over the son of the father). For a time
my emptiness was filled with grief, my vacuum transformed into
a wound.

But the vertigo returned. When death took my father it also

challenged my last authority. Nothing abides, nothing resists the acids of change and decay. I had once sought grounding in the history of Israel and in the certainties of the Christian community. That had failed me. My father had failed me by dying, he had disappointed my illusory hope—Fathers do not die! In my disappointment the question that shaped my quest was, "What can I do to give my life meaning, dignity, density?" In back of this question, no doubt, was the old Christian query, "What can I do to be saved? To be healed?"

My answer came suddenly, jumping up and down in my mind with the force of an obvious fact long denied. I woke one night in Manhattan with the words "Nothing, nothing" on my lips. As I started to laugh at the comedy of my own seriousness my vertigo began to subside. I saw that I had been obsessed with the wrong question. In the face of the uncertainty of life and the certainty of death no human act or project could render existence meaningful or secure. Nothing I could *do* would result in my being saved, ontologically grounded against tragedy and death. Either dignity and meaningfulness come with the territory or they must forever be absent. Sanctity is given with being. It is not earned. Worthiness may not be contingent; otherwise it is unattainable. I had been riding on an ox looking for an ox. With considerably lessened anxiety I ceased asking, "What must I do . . .?" and began to ask, "Who am I?"

It is more difficult to stick with the question "Who am I?" than one might imagine. Psychoanalysis led me back into the maze by suggesting that I might best answer the question by delving into the past and discovering *why* I am as I am. Thus I was back to looking for identity in history. But this time in my personal biography and not in the history of Israel. Freud promised that if I could recover the history I had repressed, if I made the unconscious conscious, I would achieve the graceful identity for which I had been searching. Religion and philosophy had failed to dispel my dis-ease; perhaps healing of the psyche might come from psychology.

Although it was an early-morning flight, my reverie was in full swing. Breakfast was finished, the tray removed by a stewardess with a perma-smile tattooed on what might have been an interesting face. I settled back and surrendered to fantasy. How many times I had made this trip in imagination! With a guide (an archaeologist of the psyche) I had explored the ecstatic and painful territory of my childhood. At first tentatively, and then with more courage, I had returned to rediscover the gifts and wounds I received in growing up. I tasted again of my loneliness, my anger and my insatiable and thwarted hunger for affection. I remembered, as well, the love homogenized into small offerings—hot chocolate after sledding and hand-embroidered pockets on a cowboy shirt.

Now, after twenty-five years' absence, I was returning to the scene of the famous rubber-gun wars (when we painted Hammy Traylor's head green and stained the Long boys' barn with glass vials of a magic liquid called "Congo Red"), to the wilderness of the College Woods where I first learned to hunt like Daniel Boone, and to smoke rabbit tobacco, and where I discovered soft, red lips that still flame in dreams. I was going back to the sacred time of innocence before decision, tragedy, and death ruled the world.

The main street of Maryville was reassuring, changed but recognizable. The funeral parlor had assumed an institutional grandeur and the bank had a new façade—acres of glass and disciplined steel beams designed to suggest friendly availability and stability (the doors still closed at 3 o'clock). But the drugstore had its same marble counter, and dark wooden chairs, and booths, etched with memories of cokes, cheese sandwiches, and hieroglyphics celebrating generations of highschool romances. The barber shop, where I once saw the shoeshine boy have a "sunstroke," seemed still to be the nerve center for minor vice. No shaves on Saturday, but information on horses and the latest edition of the *Police Gazette* were still provided with haircuts. The 10-cent-store had its customary supply of balloons still conveniently placed for young shoplifters, and I had to remind myself that it was not appropriate to repeat my child-hood ritual of stealing a few to keep on hand against hard times. I was not able to find any trace of the livery stable which had been near the jail, but as I think about it, I am not certain whether it existed in reality or whether I remembered it into existence after reading Lincoln Steffens' *Autobiography.*

Walking down streets once familiar, I wandered deeper into the heart of nostalgia. It was late afternoon when I reached the edge of the woods. The path led me by the oak trees where Robin Hood and his men met to devise a plan for sneaking into college football games, past the graveyard, down into the small valley where I once saw a bear-dog-shadow. Well into the woods, I turned onto a smaller path, met the bearded ghost of a professor who had startled me listening to the wind in the pines, and proceeded to the picnic grounds. I had arrived at the holy of holies. Nothing was changed: the log over the stream was still there, and the broken boards from the dam we built two decades ago last Saturday. And there were the vines Mowgli, Tarzan, and the Keens used to swing from tree to tree (and in times of emergency to tie up members of the Long gang who wandered into our woods). The moss on the trees (not on the north side), the husky gargle of the stream, the smell of pine needles, the wood thrush defending its perimeter with chimes, mixed their magic into a potion which further dulled my sense of time. Before and after, now and then melted into each other. In the cycle of nature there was no boundary between 1940 and 1965, only the eternal return; movement without time; change without tragedy.

I was walking almost in a trance. The moon had come up, filling the woods with a dancing orgy of light and shadows and I was ten years old and anxious to be home. But it wasn't far now. Just two short hills, over the fence, and I would be on Wilson Avenue. I could see the lights in the window and I knew Dad and Mother, Lawrence, Ruth Ann, and Jackie would

be in the living room. I was close enough to see the rope swing
on the tree in the front yard. I was almost home, almost . . . .

Suddenly a voice which seemed to echo from all around
crashed in and shattered my reverie: ". . . . race riots . . . cities
burning . . . immorality in the schools. Fellow Americans, we
have to do something about these niggers, communists, and
Jews. They're taking over the country." My trance was dispelled
immediately. The moonlight lost its enchantment, turned sour
and became sinister. The voice continued. More about conspiracy. Where was it coming from? Not from one house. The
sound was too pervasive. Perhaps all the television sets in the
neighborhood were tuned to the same channel. No. Many of
the houses were dark. Like a dog on a scent I followed the
voice in the wind. Up over the hill, down Court Street, across
the railroad tracks. As I got nearer the courthouse, the voice
became more distinct, carried now by a bull horn, not the wind.
A man was speaking from a platform surrounded by a circle of
cars. In back of him stood figures in hooded robes—white, red,
and green. Suddenly everything became clear. A Ku Klux Klan
meeting was in progress and the wind had carried the sound
over a mile, up over the hill, and dropped it on Wilson Avenue.

I walked into the circle of listeners. Speaker after speaker
repeated the litany condemning communists, niggers, Jews,
seminary professors who destroyed belief in the Bible, and the
National Council of Churches. The final speaker announced
that the meeting would climax with a cross-burning. As the
Klansmen were getting their torches ready a whispered message
went among the college students who were onlookers: "When
they light the cross form a circle and sing 'We Shall Overcome'." The first notes of our song threatened the Klansmen's
reverie, as the voice from their meeting had earlier destroyed
mine. Several of them plowed into the circle of singers with
fists swinging. The circle scattered. The police (who had been
watching the whole time) arrived, broke up the fights, and
everyone started home.

A long night followed. The Klan had stirred my anger, scorn, and disdain but had left me fully awake. As my initial violence subsided I experienced a perceptual reversal, a moment of insight when I understood that my scorn and violence were, in truth, aimed at myself. The Klansmen and I were one in philosophy. We were both living by nostalgia. Their system of meanings and models was anchored securely in an imagined past, in the myths of individualism, Americanism, fundamentalism, and white supremacy. Mine was rooted in my individual history. I was in Maryville on an archaeological expedition in quest of my past. I was hopeful of discovering on this sacred soil models for a life-style which I could adopt as my own. In fact, I had for years tried to live by the moral and religious traditions of my parents with little reverence for the uniqueness of my own experience. In the terrifying and violent anacronism of the Klan I saw clearly, for the first time, the tragedy and folly of the exile who seeks the ground of his identity in the past (either a public or a private past). The exile's past is quickly changed into a myth, a reverenced tradition, a set of authoritative models which serve to remove the burden of responsible decision from the present moment. It becomes an excuse, a flight from responsibility. When I depend upon the past for my dignity or for the models of the life-style I will adopt I become dissociated from my present. Memory rather than awareness becomes the basis of identity. I become a product, a victim of what has been, and not a free agent able to respond to what is happening now.

On the flight back I tried to sleep but could not. My reverie of the weekend had taken away my desire to dream. I was coming home to the obvious. After squandering much of my substance wandering in the future and the past I was returning to my native time—the present. I had not yet learned how to cultivate the now, to live gracefully in the present, to love the actual, but I was no longer in exile.

II | *Homecoming—*
Novelty and
the Gracefulness of Time

In fantasy and myth homecoming is a dramatic event: bands play, the fatted calf is killed, a banquet prepared, and there is rejoicing that the prodigal has returned. In reality exile is frequently ended gradually, with no dramatic, external events to mark its passing. The haze in the air evaporates and the world comes into focus; seeking gives way to finding; anxiety to satisfaction. Nothing is changed and everything is changed. Wittgenstein observed that at such times we find ourselves silent and without adequate words, because homecoming does not involve coming to know any new facts about the world but merely a changed perception. Human existence ceases to be a problem to be solved and becomes a mystery to be enjoyed. The secret is that nothing is lost. Seek and you will not find. Give up the quest for the kingdom of God and you discover the holiness of your native soil. Thus, Zen wisdom has frequently pictured the enlightened man as totally incarnate in his acts; when he eats he eats, when he sleeps he sleeps, when he fears he fears.

It may be that homecoming is the secularized or deparochialized equivalent of what Christians traditionally meant by justification by faith. For both Paul and Luther justification involved the realization that human salvation was not contingent upon any human action. No striving, no good works, no righteous style of life, no correct opinions could serve to validate human existence. In divorcing salvation from achievement, the Christian tradition established the priority of being over doing. Yet Paul and Luther still do not point a universal way beyond exile, for they made salvation depend upon appropriating an event in the past—the life, death, and resurrection of Christ. In order to appropriate this event the contemporary believer must adopt alien moral, intellectual, and philosophical categories from a time in history that is not his own. Justification by faith leaves me in exile from the historical time of my incarnate existence if it makes belief in the unique atoning work of Christ a condition of salvation. Homecoming involves the realization that gracefulness requires nothing but the individual's becoming fully incarnate in his own body and historical situation. Grace is the natural mark of a fully human life. It does not need to be conferred by Jesus Christ nor confirmed by the church.

While the description of homecoming may be less dramatic than that of exile, there nevertheless may be a phenomenological study of the structures of graceful existence in the present.

The Dis-eased Present

Perhaps the most clarifying way to begin to isolate the notion of graceful existence in the present is to describe its opposite. One form of dis-eased temporality is living in exile *from* the present, as if the present were only a way-station on the road to the future, or were merely the repetition of life patterns established in the past. The opposite pathology, which has never been my peculiar style of dis-ease, is to live in exile *in* the present, to live as if the present were the only moment of human time.

The perennial romantic conviction that authentic human existence is lived totally within the present moment is currently in strong resurgence. In the "now" generation both the study of history and careful planning for the future seem to be anathema. Neither memory nor hope attracts major investments of youthful imagination. The carelessness of adolescence has become an ideal for the "mature" adult; *The Graduate* a model of authentic action; emotional immediacy the only measure of

sincerity; *Spontaneity*—the banner of a generation. Even sophisticated thinkers such as N. O. Brown, A. Maslow, Norman
Mailer, and Fritz Perls champion the romantic ideal. Here is
Maslow's version as articulated in his concept of the creative
personality.

In the child there is a total unquestioning acceptance of whatever happens. Since there is also very little memory, very little
leaning on the past, there is little tendency in the child to bring
the past into the present or into the future. The consequence is
that the child is totally without past and future.

If one expects nothing, if one has no anticipations or apprehen-
sions, if in a certain sense there is no future, because the child is
moving totally "here-now," there can be no surprise, no disappointment. One thing is as likely as another to happen. This is
"perfect waiting" and spectatorship without any demands that one
thing happen rather than another. There is no prognosis. And no
prediction means no worry, no anxiety, no apprehension or
foreboding.

This is all related to my conception of the creative personality
as one who is totally here—now, one who lives without future or
past. Another way of saying this is: "The creative person is an
innocent." An innocent could be defined as a grown person who
can still perceive, or think, or react like a child. It is this innocence
that is recovered in the "second naivete," or perhaps I will call it
the "second innocence" of the wise old man who has managed to
recover the ability to be childlike.*

In the romantic view of time the child is taken as the model
of authentic temporality and thus the past and the future are
surgically severed from the present. The authentic man is
defined as the innocent who is virgin-born in every moment
without the contamination of memory or hope. It may be

* Abraham H. Maslow, "Innocent Cognition," Western Behavioral Science
Institute paper. Quoted in Everett Shostrom, *Man the Manipulator* (New York:
Bantam Books, Inc., 1968), p. 58.

worthwhile to note the extremes to which thought must go
to preserve this impossible ideal. Nietzsche and Dostoevski
both saw that God must be put to death before man would
be free to be without limits. Dostoevski had Ivan say, *"If* God
is dead all things are possible"; and Nietzsche took the terrifying step of proclaiming that God must be put to death in
order for man to return to the innocent sensuality that was his
birthright. So long as there is a god, there are "oughts" which
arise either from tradition or from aspiration for holiness, and
these are repressive of spontaneity. He who has loyalty to a
tradition or hope for the future still believes in God and is
not free. (See "Storytelling and the Death of God," p. 82 ff.,
for the detailing of this line of argument.)

The impossibility and the tragic consequences of living in a
perpetual present became dramatically evident to me in a recent
event. On a Saturday afternoon in early fall I was domesti-
cating, defining and privatizing my living space—constructing
a redwood fence around my back yard. A man in his early
thirties paused while walking his dog, watched me for a time,
and asked if he could help. He explained that he loved to work
with wood and had little to occupy his time. I accepted his offer
but before I could tell him when I would be working next
he interrupted me: "There is something I must tell you now
while I remember it. If I wait it may be too late. I don't know."
He went on to explain that several years before he had been
injured in an accident in which a small piece of metal had
pierced the section of his brain which stores and controls
memory. Immediately after the accident he had been rushed to
the hospital with little chance of remaining alive and less of
retaining the ability to engage in rational thought. Somehow
he survived and the long road of rehabilitation began. He had
learned to talk again with scarcely any impediment. But he
still had no control over his memory. At one time he could
remember incidents from the ancient past but could not recall
what he had said five minutes before. At other times he could

remember the recent past but not how he had been injured. Lacking a dependable memory he could not hold a job or plan for the future in spite of his technical intelligence being largely unimpaired. I listened to his story with a growing sense of tragedy. We planned to meet on the following Monday and work on the fence together but he never appeared. I imagine that he found the slip of paper on which I had written my name and address in his pocket and could not recall how it got there. Nor did I seek him out at his home for fear of the embarrassment of not being recognized. How could friendship develop where there is neither memory nor promise?

The contemporary ideal of living completely within the present moment, no less than the classical mystical notion of living totally within the eternal now of the divine presence, is as impossible as it is inhuman. It results in a dis-eased rather than a graceful present. If we define the now as the only authentic human time, we are forced to conclude that man's true home is in the Eden of childhood which is forever lost and not in civilization. Human culture differs from the associations formed by lower animals because it tempers spontaneity with wisdom inherited from the past and by hopes projected into the future. Memory and anticipation are woven into the fabric of every human action. If we seek a graceful identity we must cease to give allegiance to the romantic rhetoric which celebrates only that innocent and spontaneous action which takes place in a virgin-born present. In addition we must realize that the idealization of childhood as the model for authentic life is destructive of the dignity of mature human existence. The child that Maslow and other romantics create is as mythological as Adam. He certainly bears no relation to the little people who live in my house who remember their Grandfather with longing, anticipate birthdays, Christmas, and growing up, and are far too manipulative to engage in " 'perfect waiting' and spectatorship without any demands that one thing happen rather than another." A child is no more an adequate model of authentic adult existence than the adult is an adequate model of what a child should be (as Victorian parents assumed). When we hold up Eden as the ideal, when we praise innocence, when we celebrate only the here and now, we sacrifice the actual and potential integrity of human existence for an impossible ideal (strangely enough, this is the exact fault which Christianity committed according to Nietzsche). We become human only on leaving Eden, mature only in realizing that childhood is over. We come home to the fullness of our humanity only in owning and taking responsibility for present awareness as well as for the full measure of our memories and dreams. Graceful existence integrates present, past, and future.

The Vibrant Present

What does it mean to live vibrantly in the present? The question is both inane and profound. Just as immediate, un-prejudiced perception is at once the most natural and the most difficult human achievement, the present is both my sole possession and the last moment of my time to be fully inhabited. I am able to live fully in it only when compulsion and demand, false reverence for the past and fantastic expectations for the future have abated. To live in the present involves a shift in gravity, a greater investment of energy in awareness than in remembrance or expectation. However, full awareness takes place only where there remains a resonance with past and future.

The ambiguities of the word "present" suggest a relationship between presence, presents (gifts), and living in the present. To live in the present is to live in the presence of things, persons, and events. To be now is to be with. When someone presents himself to me I receive his presence as a gift (a datum). Thus the notion of living in the present involves the idea of living close to data or phenomena.

The first step toward a vibrant present is getting in touch

with the data which are most immediately given to awareness—
the sensations, things, persons, events, ideas, and institutions
which constitute my world. As a self I am a cosmic center from
which all lines radiate, I am the nexus where all dimensions
of reality meet. To get in touch with my sensations and
perceptions is, therefore, to know the whole world of which
I am the center.

The second step requires that I go beyond the idiosyncratic
and egocentric perceptions of immediate experience. Mature
awareness is possible only when I have digested and com-
pensated for the biases and prejudices that are the residue of
my personal history. Awareness of what presents itself to me
involves a double movement of attention: silencing the familiar
and welcoming the strange. Each time I approach a strange
object, person, or event, I have a tendency to let my present
needs, past experience, or expectations for the future determine
what I will see. If I am to appreciate the uniqueness of any
datum, I must be sufficiently aware of my preconceived ideas and
characteristic emotional distortions to bracket them long enough
to welcome strangeness and novelty into my perceptual world.
This discipline of bracketing, compensating, or silencing
requires sophisticated self-knowledge and courageous honesty.
Yet, without this discipline each present moment is only the
repetition of something already seen or experienced. In order
for genuine novelty to emerge, for the unique presence of
things, persons, or events to take root in me, I must undergo
a decentralization of the ego.

I can easily imagine a dialogue between myself and a more-
than-normally-philosophical rock in which my egocentricity is
increasingly disarmed:

SK: Damn it! Why did you trip me?

ROCK: I didn't trip you, I'm just lying here in my space con-
versing with the sky and the ground and you come up and kick
me.

SK: Well, never mind all that. I see now that you are just about the right shape and size for a wall I am building.

ROCK: First you accuse me of abusing you, but now it is clear that you are the aggressor who is lacking in regard for me. You still haven't seen me. All you can see is a use to which I may be put. Why don't you exercise your facility of wonder for a moment.

SK: I suppose I could try. What would you like me to do?

ROCK: Look at the nuances of color in me, for a beginning. Then you might notice the gracefulness of my form (far too fine to be hidden in a wall). Finally, if you can muster sufficient imagination, run your hands fondly over me and feel my massed energy and at least ask yourself the fantastic question of what my reality is like from the inside . . . . Well—what do you think? You seem rather silent.

SK: When I take the time to look at you from different perspectives to welcome your strangeness into my consciousness I am both rewarded and confused. I see your beauty now and not merely your usefulness. But I still have a wall to build. Any suggestions?

ROCK: No. I don't know how you can solve the dilemma of both reverencing and utilizing, but I know that once you have welcomed me into your awareness you will not be so simple-minded as to suppose rocks and trees exist only to trip you or as raw materials for constructing walls and houses. Next time you come this way you might even look to keep from disturbing my rest.

Only rarely do such philosophical stones present themselves to me in such a disarming manner. I am more frequently startled by becoming aware of the mystery of persons who have long been intimate friends or enemies. A moment of lucidity may emerge in confronting an old acquaintance (like a tongue of wind blowing the fog from a single cove of a wooded shore) in which I suddenly see the projections and the distortions that I have brought to our previous meetings. Bracketing these for a moment, I see before me a person previously unknown in spite of many encounters. How many years it has taken me to see my wife without the imposition of images of my mother, other women I have known, the archetypal women, or the ideal wife conjured up by my hostile imagination! As I come into fuller possession of my past and my characteristic modes of projecting, I become gradually more innocent and spontaneous in my perceptions and actions. As I take back what I have imposed upon others I receive more fully the gifts they are willing to offer. Repentance precedes homecoming. I come into the presence of another only when I have recognized, accepted, and made amends for the cognitive sins I have committed in choosing to see my neighbor only as an example, a problem, an instance, or a means of satisfying my own need.

Thus freedom lies on the far side of discipline; the present may only be inhabited by the man who lives in full resonance with his past and future; awareness is complete only when it vibrates with memory and expectation; spontaneity belongs only to the person who has taken responsibility for his projections; innocence is recovered only after compulsion has been recognized. Freedom, seasoned innocence, spontaneity, novelty, living in the present are marks of maturity which are gained only by the long process of finding one's way back from the exile which culture, ignorance, and cowardice impose upon us all.

This ability to experience novelty, to perceive freshly, to be surprised may well be one of the defining marks of human dignity. In those moments when I am able to rise above compulsion, need, and expectation and allow some novelty to refresh me, I am most certain of my freedom and my potency. I become gracefully free when I become convinced that I have the power to do a new thing. Hannah Arendt has forged the connection between novelty, freedom, action, potency, and grace in a manner I have found unforgettable:

The life span of man running toward death would inevitably carry everything to ruin and destruction if it were not for the faculty of interrupting it and beginning something new, a faculty which is inherent in action like an ever-present reminder that men, though they must die, are not born in order to die but in order to begin . . . .

The miracle that saves the world, the realm of human affairs, from its normal "natural" ruin is ultimately the fact of natality, in which the faculty of action is ontologically rooted. It is, in other words, the birth of new men and the new beginning, the action they are capable of by virtue of being born. Only the full experience of this capacity can bestow on human affairs faith and hope.*

Every man has his Bethlehem where new possibilities and hopes are born, where his history is invaded by novelty and the potency for new action. At such times the tyranny of the past and the terror of the future give way before a new time of open possibility—the vibrant present.

The Living Past

Like most of my contemporaries, I have been nurtured by two incompatible views of history: the Judeo-Christian notion of an objective past which contains an indispensable revelation of the truth, and the pragmatic, ahistorical tradition which considers history "bunk" (Henry Ford) and of no consequence for present existence. Both of these philosophies view history as a series of events which is objectively fixed beyond alteration. The past may be either worshiped or ignored but it may not be changed. Neither view has prepared me for what I experience

* Hannah Arendt, *The Human Condition* (Garden City: Doubleday Anchor Book, 1958), p. 222.

as I live more completely within a vibrant present—the openness of the past to novelty.

Perhaps the central failure of the Christian and the pragmatic views of history lies in their understanding of memory on the model of a camera—memory may pick the events it will preserve but it records them with an objective lens. Psychoanalysis has made us aware of the error of this analogy. Memory as it functions in the normal, alienated individual, far from being an accurate historical record has the function of preserving the economy and harmony of the psyche. It operates under guidelines which are set forth by the superego and enforced by the censors of the ego. The past which we remember is partial and distorted; it has been edited by the censors to exclude events which are disturbingly painful or disturbingly pleasurable. The memories of our early ecstasy and pain, intimate communion and utter abandonment, deep wounds and gracious gifts have been blunted or repressed. The history we recall tends to be propaganda which preserves the status quo of personal identity. It creates heroes and villains, gods and demons out of mortal flesh in order to have authorities to whom the responsibility for the agony of decision may be surrendered and targets for hostility which otherwise would have to be recognized as self-hatred. The censor of memory is the internal "grand inquisitor" who keeps the personality dependent upon miracle, mystery, and authority rather than allow it to face the anxiety of free and responsible existence. To the degree that the grand inquisitor functions within the personality, the history we remember is mythological. A mythological history regards the structures of personality and society as having been established by events or persons (divine or human) which are remote and beyond the control of the presently existing individual. This mythological past is static and closed. It consists of "once-upon-a-time" events, such as the Oedipus complex or the resurrection, which provide the unalterable foundation of identity.

So long as I looked to my past for the authoritative models which would give shape to my existence, I remained a boy living in a world of adults who had almost Godlike power. I created the myth of parents who were responsible for the joys and pains, the beliefs and values which accompanied me as a pseudo-Israelite living in exile. For the succor they provided me I owed them a loyalty that bordered on worship. For their failure to love me with ever-present, never-failing, completely understanding, absolutely unselfish devotion they deserved my righteous anger. For it is clear to the childish self that parents, being omnipotent beings, can disappoint their creatures only willfully. Gods never fail accidentally, or from fatigue, or from limited wisdom, or from being preoccupied with their own pain or need.

As I increasingly refuse to be an exile, a victim, an alien in a strange land, and come to inhabit the here and now, I discover myself as a responsible agent. My mythological past is destroyed, my censors relax, and I begin to recover a past that I had never known. My ancient gods become mortals. My temples are converted into museums, my authorities into guideposts, my models into companions, my gurus into friends. As I recognize my complicity in the decisions which have given shape to my life, I cease to view myself as a victim of my history, as a fated product of my environment. Even as a child I chose the manner in which I would respond to the gifts and demands of my environment. When I assume the responsibility for my style of life, my parents cease being mythological and become incarnate. I discover the ambivalence of my familiar history, its passion and partiality, failures and triumphs, weaknesses and strengths. I know, for the first time, the agony and the courage which was the ambiance of my childhood. Worship of the gods is replaced by reverence for human dignity.

When I demythologize my past and recognize the ambivalent and tragic character of all human action, I discover a new freedom to change the significance of what has been. So long as I was a victim of my past I could only rebel against it or accept it and resent those who imposed it upon me. However, as a responsible agent I am free to sift the values, attitudes, and models which are my legacy from the past and to reject those which are alien to my present experience and affirm those which are compatible.

This also means I am able to distinguish between wounds which have been inflicted upon me and gifts which have been given, and to react with the appropriate attitudes—forgiveness and gratitude. If I have been injured by severity or indifference, by being loved too little, too much, or unwisely, I become free from these wounds only when I recognize them and forgive the persons responsible for inflicting them. If I have been overly dependent upon my father I will seek out authorities to reverence and obey. If I resent my mother's conditional love (the Oedipus situation), I will project her face upon other women in order to retain a ready target for my anger. Forgiveness alone allows me both to accept my past and to be free from its crippling wounds. Hatred binds me in a repetition compulsion, in a continual search for targets (or its opposite— paranoia—the conviction that I am a universal target). In gratitude I am able to affirm my continuity with my past and to retain voluntarily those gifts which are integral to my on-going identity. Thus I am able at once to judge that the early demand made upon me for conformity to orthodox Christian beliefs marked me with certain rigidities, with an excess of seriousness, and with an uncomfortably strong need to be right; to understand and forgive the failure in wisdom of those who made this demand; and to give thanks for the Christian-pilgrim style of life which keeps me gypsying in search of new meanings, new epiphanies of the sacred. Judgment, forgiveness, and gratitude perform the alchemy which transforms the past from fate into fortune and which changes me from being a victim of causes over which I had no control to being a par-

ticipant in a past which I continually re-form. They introduce
novelty, and therefore life, into what has been previously a
dead past.

The Open Future

A graceful future is one open to psychological, political, and
ontological novelty. It emerges naturally from a life-style which
centers in awareness of the vibrant present. Such openness is
properly called "hope," and it rests upon the intuition of the
novel possibilities resident in all life. Despair rests upon the
opposite perception—the view that any possible future is a
mere repetition of the past.

The openness of my future does not preclude aspiring and
planning. To the contrary, it strengthens my impulse to take
responsibility for designing and working toward the most
satisfying future I can imagine because I am convinced of
the potency of human action to create novelty. The passivity
and despair which is painfully central in *Waiting for Godot*
and in so much adolescent, posturing nihilism roots in and
contributes to human impotence. It rests upon the conviction
that man is no longer sufficiently potent to render the future
pregnant with novel possibilities; therefore he may only wait
for the inevitable. To the degree that I am aware of the novel
and satisfying possibilities in the present, I will make plans
and take steps to actualize these possibilities in the future.
Being in a vibrant present means acting toward some chosen
future. The joy I experience, for instance, in clearing land I
own on an island in Maine of the tangled underbrush
which remains from a pulp-cutting operation is inseparable
from the anticipated satisfaction I have of continuing to enjoy
the beauty of the land for years to come. My satisfaction arises
jointly from present enjoyment and future promise.

The chief difference between a dis-eased and an open future
is that the anticipating and planning I do in the latter does not

have to come to fruition in order for my identity to be established. When my center of gravity, my major capital investment of energy and attention is in the present, I do not count upon any future event to ratify, justify, or dignify my existence. My worth is not contingent upon the coming of the kingdom of God, the establishment of the classless society, or writing the definitive essay on time. My identity is secured by my awareness of the resident sacredness of the present moment of time. I *am* here and now. Although I hope that I will continue to grow toward a richer and more satisfying style of life, there is no future perfection I must achieve before I may accept myself. What I plan is an extension of what I desire. My projected future is primarily a concrete means of taking responsibility for continuing satisfaction, not a program for repaying debts or fulfilling obligations.

The time for ending has come. I am again aware of the clock: tick, tick, tick, tick, tick, tick. I easily become caught up in its cadence and the anxiety begins to rise within me. I am tempted to escape into fixity. Have I learned nothing in thinking through my experience of time that may provide an antidote to fear and the desire to escape? As I ask, I become aware of a new sound invading my space: boom, boom, boom, boom, boom, boom; the waves march in and hurl themselves against the sand, and bass-drum thunder strikes the land at irregular intervals. Gradually the rhythms of land and sea syncopate, clock sounds and water sounds vibrate together (like the breathing of lovers) boom, tick, boom, tick, boom tick tick, boom, tick, tick, boom tick, boom tick. I relax and am invaded by the syncopated rhythm; my times are inserted within the tides of the sea; knowledge and mystery, *chronos* and *kairos,* time and eternity begin to dance together. As my anxiety is dissolved, the moments of my time begin to move freely and harmoniously; memory and anticipation interweave with awareness. Moonlight parties and early love on beaches a continent and a generation away and dreams of a cabin on the evergreen shore of Swan's Island wash together and swirl around with California sand. I am at home in my times: satisfied to be in this place; grateful to have known the wilderness of Tennessee mountains and the ordered calm of Harvard Yard; and—yes—the desert of Palestine which at times flows with milk and honey; pleasantly awaiting the ripening of dreams and the birth of surprises. The ticking still goes on. Its relentless rhythm sometimes seems to drown out the pounding of the waves and anxiety threatens to overwhelm me. But I think I know, now, that exile is chosen and therefore it is always possible to come home again.

Grace is the courage to be at home in the moving resonance of the present.

TWO | *Education for Serendipity*

Long ago, when I wore short pants and shot marbles with my left hand, I formed an impression of education which has recently returned to haunt me. Mrs. Jones' first-grade classroom always seemed dark, but on this particular day it was more depressing than usual. For an eternal afternoon I sat practicing my penmanship exercises, listening to Mrs. Jones' monotone: "Make your *i*'s come all the way up to the middle line. And don't forget to make your *o*'s nice and round. Circle, circle, circle. Period. Now repeat." Caught somewhere between boredom and despair I struggled against tears and settled in to wait for the resurrection—the 3:00 o'clock bell.

And then it happened. A movement in a tree outside the window caught my eye and there, in the sweet and redeeming light of the springtime world, was a summer warbler building a nest. Caught in wonder I followed the progress of the nest construction and dreamt of the time when I would be a great ornothologist. My *i*'s and *o*'s were forgotten until Mrs. Jones materialized over my shoulder and demanded to know why three lines in my penmanship book were empty. Instinct warned me that no serendipitous warbler, no private fascination, could provide an excuse for the neglect of my serious educational duties. So I bit my tongue, cherished my wonder in silence, and stayed in after school to make up my lessons.

Mrs. Jones won more than the day. Schooling became a habit for me and I remained in the classroom for twenty-five years and five degrees without seriously questioning the maxim that private enthusiasm must be divorced from the educational task. In college and graduate school my attention was focused upon the ideas that are considered the necessary working capital of the educated man. I was introduced to theological, philosophical, biological, psychological, anthropological, and sociological models of man. I learned methodologies for solving cognitive problems, and techniques for discovering the universal message in the particular text. I studied the rules of evidence and verification and learned to penetrate to the layer of doubt which lay beneath each surface certainty given me by family and culture. Although it was nowhere explicitly stated, I found the motto of education to be: *Dubito ergo sum* (I doubt therefore I am). And for years I sat with cramped muscles in hardwood chairs (with initials carved in them) and listened to lectures on the necessity for dialogue (no one laughed) and on the incarnate and engaged character of human existence.

Scarcely ever in my quarter of a century of schooling was I invited to consider the intimate, personal questions which were compelling my attention outside the classroom. While I was taught to hunt down the general, the universal, the abstract, and the public facts of the exterior world, it was tacitly assumed that education had no responsibility for helping me come to terms with the particular, the concrete, the idiosyncratic, the biographical, and the sensuous facts which formed the substance of my private existence. I learned little about the organization, appreciation, management, and care of that unique piece of human real estate which bears the legal name Sam Keen.

It is not surprising that when I finally left the classroom I could dot my *i*'s and make my *o*'s round. But the warbler was gone. I emerged from graduate school to discover that I was empty of enthusiasm. I had a profession but nothing to profess, knowledge but no wisdom, ideas but few feelings. Rich in techniques but poor in convictions, I had gotten an education but lost an identity. As I shifted my vocation from being a student concerned with possessing and organizing ideas to being a man in search of the wisdom necessary for living with vividness I came to focus on questions I had not been trained to consider, to cherish abilities which had not been cultivated, and to explore feelings which had long remained dormant. Now, finally, after too many years I have found my tongue and am talking back to Mrs. Jones.

In her defense it must be stated that Mrs. Jones had a theory of education which is deeply rooted in democratic ideology and practice. Had she articulated the principles upon which she operated she might have said something like the following: "As a teacher I must make a strict separation between the public and the private, the factual and the emotional, the objective and the subjective. Education in public schools in a democracy has no right to invade the privacy of emotions, values, or religious beliefs of individual students. A teacher must stick to those matters which can be communicated to the pupil in an antiseptic, objective manner. The principle of the separation of church and state implies that public education may not deal with matters of value which are inseparable from subjective, emotional, biographical, and religious commitment. The quest for wisdom, for identity, for ecstasy, like summer warblers, must remain outside the classroom."

On both personal and educational grounds I am convinced that Mrs. Jones' philosophy of education is dangerously wrong. I take it that education has two primary foci: it must initiate the young into the accumulated wisdom and techniques of culture, and it must prepare the young to create beyond the past, to introduce novelty, to utilize freedom. Creativity always involves an interplay between id and ego, strange and familiar, remote and proximate, universal and particular, abstract and concrete. If education neglects the intimate, the proximate, the sensuous, the autobiographical, the personal, it fails in its creative task and becomes only conservative, or perhaps reactionary. To keep a proper balance between conservation and revolution, education must deal with the intimate roots of the experience of creativity.

The revolutionary function of education is in continual danger of being submerged because it is always the generation with vested interests in the old that is in charge of educating the young. Novelty always comes as a threat. The new makes its way precariously up-stream against the current of tradition. In a democratic society the older generation conserves its values most effectively by forming a conspiracy of silence, by prohibiting the crucial questions from arising. The repressive, the reactionary function of the educational system is not so much what is done in schools as what is not done. The vacuum rather than the whip is the instrument of preserving the status quo. The whip, sooner or later, creates a rebellion which has the effect of binding the rebel to the value alternatives which are conceivable within the system against which he is rebelling. The true revolution could only be created by asking the central question of the meaning of human existence from a perspective which is alien to both the establishment and those who are locked in rebellion against the establishment. Freedom lies beyond conformity or rebellion.

I would like to propose that every educational institution, if it is to fulfill its central purpose of conserving and creating, should establish a department of "Wonder, Wisdom, and Serendipitous Knowledge" which would be charged with the prophetic task of discovering the unfashionable questions which are not being asked and the life options which are not being explored' within the educational system. In the university such a department would study the university. It would look at its rhetoric, its ideology, and its performance. It might offer courses in antique virtues, strange potentialities, and odd patterns of personal and corporate life. Certainly it should make students aware of the options, life-styles, and questions which are considered disrespectable, out of fashion, outgrown, simplistic, taboo, dangerous, or politically forbidden. It might even be well for the government to set up a new cabinet position devoted to raising embarrassing questions, considering neglected alternatives, and dramatizing different models of the fully human community. When a nation gets to the ridiculous position of spending more than half of its substance in creating new technologies of death, when it measures its power by the capacity for meta-deaths, it is by no means foolish to ask what kind of power resides in love, or in flowers. It is well to remember that Ferdinand the bull developed a response to aggression which ended in his being neither red, dead, nor armed to the teeth.

In the remainder of this chapter I will sketch out some of the courses which might be offered in a department of Wonder, Wisdom and Serendipitous Knowledge. These courses stress the conative and affective domains of education which Mrs. Jones ignored. They represent an effort to focus curriculum upon the problems and questions which I have found to be central in the years since I ended my schooling and started my education. I would not want to argue that the cognitive, abstract, scientific, disciplines which currently dominate our schools should be thrown out and education focused wholly upon development of the individual. However the time seems ripe to recover the personalistic (as opposed to the mere humanistic) dimension of education. If we neglect to educate for identity and wholeness our abstract and technological knowledge will only form a shell around a painful vacuum. I should add that the listing of courses reflects more areas of need than exact educational techniques for satisfying these needs. It is more a catalogue of experiments which need doing than a syllabus of instructions.

SILENCE, WONDER, AND THE ART OF SURRENDER

AIM. This course will explore the basic attitude which ancient philosophers insisted was the prerequisite for all wisdom —the attitude of wonder. It will aid students to develop an inner silence, to cultivate the ability to let things happen, to welcome, to listen, to allow, to be at ease in situations in which surrender rather than striving for control is appropriate.

RATIONALE. By the time a student reaches what we insist upon calling "higher" education (why not "deeper"?), his patterns of perception and style of life have been rigidly shaped by the linguistic climate in which he has been immersed since birth. Learning to speak is the model and principle of all education, since language is the earliest tool used to cut up, structure, and control the chaos of reality. The language system of a culture therefore incarnates the values and beliefs into which the child must be initiated if he is to become a man. Currently we are so anxious to accomplish this initiation before rebellion may set in that a major educational preoccupation has become how early we can teach Johnny to read, how fast and economically we can get the accumulated data of culture programed into his head (read, computer.) Since Sputnik, childhood is in danger of becoming a national resource, a warehouse for stockpiling data necessary for furthering the aims of a cybernated society.

It is difficult to avoid the impression that Western culture has formed a conspiracy against silence. Words and noise are everywhere. Our education is dominantly verbal, conceptual, and dialectic. We read, or listen, or watch, in order to be entertained. The verbal diarrhea of disc jockeys pours from the omnipresent transistor into the waiting ears of millions. Chatter fills every corner into which silence might creep. Even what we call thinking is most often a highly refined form of inner conversation. Dialectic is dialogue with an invisible partner.

A psychoanalysis of chatter would suggest that our over-verbalization is an effort to avoid something which is fearful—silence. But why should silence be threatening? Words are a way of structuring, manipulating, and controlling; thus, when they are absent the specter of loss of control arises. If we cannot name it we cannot control it. Naming gives us power. Hence silence is impotence, the surrender of control. Control is power, and power is safety. Being out of control is impotence and danger—so, at least, our fear warns us. Thus we avoid silence in order to preserve the illusion that we live in a world we control and to avoid confronting our fear of being out of control.

This obsession with controlling which characterizes technological culture blinds us to the necessity for alternative styles of perception and life. If we are unable to surrender control, to appreciate, to welcome, to wonder, to allow things and persons to speak with their own voice, to listen, we are condemned to perpetual aggression, to an unrelaxing Promethean effort to master the environment. No doubt there is a time for speaking, for dialectic, for control. But there is also a time for silence, for wonder, for surrender. It is this time we are in danger of forgetting in the contemporary world.

CONTENT AND TECHNIQUES. A course in the art of silence would, by definition, be difficult to teach. Would there be lectures, readings? How would we judge what learning had taken place? How would we grade improved skill in wondering? Where, indeed, would we find professors of silence, and how would we establish criteria for their promotion? (Perhaps those who published would be punished.) Although the difficulties are legion, it is helpful to remember that there are precedents for this experiment. Zen masters were professors of silence. By the use of koans they destroyed the naïve faith of their pupils in the final adequacy of words and concepts to grasp reality, and by meditation they taught techniques by which the mind could be emptied of dialectic without losing awareness. The testimony of Zen is that once the art of interior silence is learned, control of the interior and exterior worlds may be maintained or surrendered at will. In the Western philosophical tradition there is also precedent for education in the art of silence. Platonism, Christian mysticism, and romanticism cultivated and valued the attitudes of wonder and silent appreciation.

A course in silence might, simply, begin with silence. Imposing a period of linguistic asceticism would sensitize students to the omnipresence of words and the threat of silence. It would foster the awareness that words and silence, ideas and feelings, concepts and sensations, controlling and surrendering, remain vital only so long as they are in continual relationship. Coming home to speaking after a sojourn in silent exile, a student might have gained sufficient reverence for language to become outraged at chatter, propaganda, and noise. Perhaps a new revolution might emerge which would insist upon the right to silence.

Many of the meditation techniques developed in the Zen tradition, which are currently being explored at Esalen and other centers devoted to the study of the "non-verbal humanities" (Aldous Huxley), would be useful to the student of silence. With practice it is possible to observe the stream of consciousness without interferring, to silence dialectic and become aware without self-consciousness, to experience greater immediacy and spontaneity than in "normal" consciousness. The "doors of perception" may be cleansed, silence may be recovered, the art of surrendering control may be learned.

It would also be necessary to explore our nonverbal ways of learning and communicating. We rely on speech because we are never systematically trained to communicate in any other way. Yet it is clear that much is said without words. Touch, taste, and smell are largely uneducated in our culture, although they are far more intimate organs of knowledge than hearing or seeing. Getting in touch, educating the more intimate senses might help to fill the vacuum within and between persons which now is cluttered with words. We might then, as they say in Maine, speak only when we could improve on silence.

INTRODUCTION TO CARNALITY

AIM. The intent of this course is to help students experience a deeper integration between body, mind, and world, to develop a life-style richly infused with sensual and kinesthetic awareness, and to discover the sustaining certainties which arise from fully rooted and incarnate existence.

RATIONALE. Contemporary rhetoric gives all glory to flesh and matter. The combined impact of pragmatism, existentialism, scientific methodology, and the fruits of the technological revolution have convinced us that man's true home is in the kingdom of the body. The older idealistic view which saw man as a mind to which a body was accidentally attached, a spirit sadly encased in matter, is all but universally rejected in the twentieth century.

It is only in practice, never in theory, that idealistic and gnostic dualism remains a working presupposition of contemporary society. Our hymns of praise cannot drown out the hatred of the flesh which our actions reveal. Consider, for instance, our carelessness of the body in the educational process. Minds, not bodies, are taught in the classroom. At no point in the curriculum is an effort made to help students learn to read the language of the body, to acquire techniques of relaxation and control, to understand the relationship between body and personality structure, "character armor" (Reich) and defense mechanisms, motion and emotion. Our schools function as if the fact of incarnation was incidental to the task of education. Sometimes attention to the body sneaks in through courses in "personal hygiene," but these usually are a cross between internal plumbing, sex education, and edifying lessons on the value of cleanliness. What we call physical education most often consists of a series of competitive games (in season) which actually desensitize the body by focusing attention on the competitive goal of winning rather than increasing kinesthetic awareness.

The result of the hidden idealistic assumptions of our educational system is the perpetuation of a dualism, not unlike gnosticism, which separates mind from body, spirit from flesh, and appearance from feeling. The most painful symptom of this disease (a culturally condoned form of schizophrenia) is the twin phenomena of style and cosmetics. The body which displays clothing according to what is stylish is designed to be seen by others. Its dignity is in being seen, not in feeling. *Esse est percipi*. Likewise the face which is "made up" is a mask created by Helena Rubenstein which must be put on. It is a mirror face, not a flesh face, constructed with constant reference to how it will be viewed from without. To the degree that we design our bodies to be seen, we are divorced from the perspective of carnal feeling. Our education cannot be absolved of responsibility for perpetuating this style of bodily existence in which there is dominance of the visual body over the sensual body. If our bodies are hollow shells to be painted and decorated it is because we have never cared enough to educate the sensitive core; we have not undertaken to resurrect the body from deadness.

It may also be the case that the neglect of the body lies at the root of the political problem of the deterioration of the sense of public responsibility. The notion of public space is meaningful only in contrast to what is not public space, namely, private space. And the model of privacy is my relationship with my body. If I lack a sense of the density and inviolability of my own body I will have weak ego boundaries and an impaired ability to enter into social relationships. The extreme example of this simultaneous disintegration of private and public space is in the schizophrenic who lacks the feeling of being connected with his body. His body is weightless and transparent. It can be blown away by the wind or seen through by all eyes. It has no limits, boundaries, no privacy. Thus the schizophrenic child fears that his every thought and feeling can be read by the parent. There is no secret place, no fertile darkness in which tender things may take root and grow, hidden from prying eyes. Lacking a sense of potent incarnation, the schizophrenic also lacks the ability to be a member of a community. Privacy and community are related as the physical body is to the body politic. Without incarnation there is no incorporation. Embodiment is indivisible. The question is not (as the right wing insists) whether we will educate individuals to respect the integrity of private space, or (as the left wing insists) whether we will educate the community to re-create a sense of public space and responsibility. But whether we will do both, or neither. Carnal education is political and vice versa.

CONTENT AND TECHNIQUES. There is a wealth of theoretical material from physiology, psychology, and philosophy which might serve as a prelude to the study of incarnate existence. Knowledge of the basics of anatomy and physiology, not of the human body but of my body, would be a good starting point. Once a factual foundation has been provided, a physiosomatic study might draw heavily upon Freud's theory of repression and Wilhelm Reich's theory of character armor. Phenomenological analyses of the body, such as have been made by Marcel, Sartre, and Merleau-Ponty would also be valuable.

It might also be useful to reflect upon the history and sociology of the body. McLuhan has pointed out that the balance between the senses changes to compensate for the dominant technology of a given age. It is also clear that different senses have provided the models for our understanding of what it means to know. Knowledge in Greek culture, as in idealistic philosophy, was likened to seeing. To know was to have a vision or a clear and distinct idea which corresponded to the reality known. In Hebrew culture, knowing was more often understood as a mode of touch and involvement. It is no accident that the biblical tradition speaks of knowing in the sexual sense in which a man "knows" a woman. There is, at any rate, sufficient "hard" conceptual, historical, psychological, and philosophical material demonstrating the way in which the body constitutes knowledge to render a course in carnality academically respectable (if that is a concern).

The difficulty lies not with the theoretical but with the visceral dimensions of this course. Education for carnality cannot evade the problem of sex (see also the course, "Becoming a Lover," p. 57) which is at once a moral, religious, and political problem. How are we to deal with our sexuality? It is most often assumed that if we are to retain civilization we must pay the price of repression. Norman Brown and Herbert Marcuse have raised questions about this ancient presupposition which demand consideration if the revolutionary promise of education is to be fulfilled. Our genital preoccupation represents one possible form of organizing energy and time, of structuring the concerns of the body. Both Brown and Marcuse suggest that sexual, personal, and political organization are all open to change. They are matters of choice. Thus, if education aims at creating or revealing the freedom necessary to change, it would necessarily need to sensitize students to the manner in which their energies are organized. Education which avoids the erogenous zones, the sensitive areas, neglects the power structure. It would seem self-evident that if education avoids the question of power and change, it more properly deserves the name "indoctrination," and has no place in a democratic society. A democratic form of political organization distributes power and therefore consistently demands a style of bodily existence in which erotic sensibility is homogenized into the total body rather than localized in representative genital organs. It may be that a democratic society can only survive in a sensitive milieu. It is significant that the most serious revolutionary threat America has confronted in the universities arises in a time of free sexuality. It is not against the repressive superego that forbids free genital sexuality that the rebellion is directed, but against the careless pollution, desecration, and insensitive killing of the loveless technological society. The new demands are not for sex but love, not for new tyrants but participatory democracy, not for a greater share of the wealth but a more caring society. It is difficult to avoid the conclusion that the fundamental question education must deal with in the coming years is the question of alternative ways of organizing the energy and power of the physical and the political body.

There are many techniques which could be used to increase awareness of the inseparability of body, psyche, and world. Fritz Perls, the father of Gestalt therapy, has suggested a series of exercises which might form an introduction to the art of reading the language of the body. He maintains that if we single out and pay attention to any of the fundamental conscious bodily functions, such as eating, eliminating, or making love, we can construct a model of the personality. How, for instance do you eat? How do you take the world into yourself? Do you choose food carefully for its aesthetic and nutritional value? Do you pay attention to taste and texture? Chew carefully? Read when eating? As you incorporate nourishment, so you will take in and digest the world which surrounds you. If you doubt this, give full attention to your style of eating for one week and try drawing parallels to the way in which you read, listen, think, understand, and relate to persons.

Many techniques for educating and resensitizing the body might also be borrowed from therapeutic and religious disciplines. Eastern religions have centuries of experience in educating the body which to date have not been taken seriously by Western educators. It is possible to separate the idealistic metaphysics and the presuppositions of Eastern spirituality from yoga practices and make use of its technology of body awareness and control. One example of how this might be done: the Zen technique of focusing attention upon breathing provides an immediate experimental basis for understanding and integrating the involuntary and the voluntary; it provides a bodily model of the tension between unconscious and conscious functions of the personality. The moment one *tries* to breathe spontaneously it becomes obvious that it is futile to try to make happen those things which can only be allowed to happen. Enlightenment (the state at which education aims) consists in being able to discern the appropriate moments for acceptance and action, wonder and work, relaxation and willfulness. It should be obvious that this ability is a prerequisite for happiness so long as man must both accept the limits of mortality and strive to extend his control.

Another ancient educational medium which might be revived is dance. In primitive cultures dance was a central way of exhibiting and celebrating values and beliefs. As Arthur Darby Nock, the Harvard historian of religions, was fond of saying, "Primitive religion is not believed. It is danced." Even Plato knew that dance and gymnastics were essential for political education; if the values of a culture are to be deeply rooted they must be celebrated with all the facilities—reason, emotion, and sensation. The body has wisdom to teach that the mind knows not of. It understands much of rhythm and timing which is easily forgotten when life is ruled too exclusively by ideas. Such fundamental themes as the relation between activity and passivity, strength and weakness, tension and relaxation, disease and grace are more easily learned from bodily movement

than from conceptual analysis. As Zorba knew, there are times
when only dance can say what must be said. There are certain
emotions which are difficult to entertain without motion. We
are moved by joy, or shaken by grief. It may be that the sparsity
of joy in contemporary life is closely related to the loss of
dance as a central vehicle for the education and articulation
of values and beliefs. We do not share the same dances.
Perhaps corporate bonds are strongly forged only when bodies
join together in celebration. If so, re-education of the body is
essential for creating a community. Is it really possible to be
in touch without touching, to be moved without moving?

HOW TO TELL TIME:
THE USES OF SUNDIALS, CALENDARS, AND
CLOCKS

AIM. This course is a study of a variety of ways in which
human time is structured, measured, and understood. It is concerned equally with the history of each understanding and with
helping the student identify in his own experience the basis for
the differing notions of time. It aims at existential clarification
of the difference between being prompt and being timely
(chronos and kairos).

RATIONALE. The industrial revolution began symbolically
with the invention of the portable clock, when the tick-tock
of mechanical chronology replaced the sun and the passing
seasons as the index of time. In the era of the sundial, the
rhythm of desire and satisfaction, planting and harvest, energy
and fatigue encouraged human action to break forth in the
time of ripeness. *Kairos* rather than *chronos,* the prepared
moment rather than the correct moment governed life. The
clock is now grafted into the psyche and replaces the rhythms
of the body and nature with the prefabricated cadence of the
metronome. We march to the beat of an alien pacemaker,
eating when the clock strikes 8, 12, and 6, working five times

eight hours per week, and retiring from labor at age sixty-five.

And who can deny that it is well for trains to run on schedule, for meetings to begin promptly, for efficiency to be measured by time studies? Each of us has but a limited time to inhabit the earth and should it not be used profitably? By ordering time in abstract modules we have gained the regularity necessary to live with the machines we have created. And we have been rewarded with what we unquestionably consider "a higher standard of living." But what have we lost in the transition?

Perhaps when we ceased to measure time by the sun and the seasons, it was wisdom that suffered, the sense of the organic rhythm of birth, maturation, and death which governs all life. There is an ancient tradition which defines wisdom as the sense of timeliness and appropriateness. Ecclesiastes states the point well: "For everything there is a season, and a time for every matter under heaven": the wise man knows what time it is in his own life and in the life of the community (see *Apology for Wonder* for elaboration of this point). Education, which aims at wholeness, must teach a man to tell time.

CONTENT AND TECHNIQUE. A course in how to tell time might begin with a study of sundials and the cyclical view of time. This view of time dominated the human consciousness (with the possible exception of the Hebrew-Christian mind) until the birth of technology. There are two sources of this view: the cycle of the seasons and the human unconscious. In nature there is no finality, only an endless process of change. Nothing is ever lost. What has been remains as the soil of the present. Death and decay form the humus which nurtures the new life that is always reaching for a strange yet eternal future. Change and permanence are curiously wed in the perennial mystery of the dying and resurrecting earth. And so it is, also, in the depths of the human psyche. In dreams the living and the dead dwell together without prejudice of the reality principle. The child that I was, insatiably hungry for love, remains unrequited, still pleading and longing in spite of the myriad satisfactions of adult affection. Now and then, here and there, the possible and the impossible, past, present and future, symbol and fact—all join together in the dance. And nothing is forgotten, lost, dead. All that ever was or will be remains a living possibility.

Contact with the seasonal reality of nature and with the unconscious is essential for hope—the confidence that although all things change, death is not the final reality which defines the human spirit. To gain some sense of participation in the natural order, to be swept away momentarily into "the oceanic consciousness" (Freud), or to experience union with what mystics have described as the All gives courage to create with the confidence that nothing is ever lost. Creativity, the incarnation of hope in action, depends upon continual intercourse between id and ego, unconscious and conscious, the cyclical-archaic and the linear-chronological senses of time.

The second variety of temporal understanding involves calendars and the linear sense of time. If we focus upon the cycle of nature or on the human unconscious, the circle appears to be the appropriate model for time. However, from the perspective of the individual, time is a straight line stretched between birth and death, an arrow that flies ever toward a new future, a road which does not bend back upon itself. Marshall McLuhan notwithstanding, the linear fashion of thinking about time stems primarily from taking the essential mortality of human life seriously and not from the invention of the alphabet.

All cultures have created ways of punctuating the calendars of individual and corporate existence. Since the people, like the land, abide there are yearly festivals and holidays celebrating the changing seasons. And for the individual there are rites of passage which mark the transition from one period of life into the next. By dramatizing birth, coming of age, marriage, childbirth, death, and other hinge-points, primitive rites of passage eased the burden of change by inserting the individual within the context of a universal process. The calendar imposed a common structure on time and thus did much to alleviate loneliness by providing regular moments for shared celebration and grief.

In our pluralistic society we are rapidly losing common punctuation points. Our holidays, like our rites of passage, are becoming diffuse. Birth and death are accomplished in antiseptic isolation, childhood is lost before schooling ends, and maturity is, hopefully, born in the identity struggles of the thirties and forties. Erik Erikson has made it clear that there are standard crisis points in the identity cycle, traumas which must be negotiated successfully before a higher stage of personality development may be reached. However, we lack appropriate rituals for socializing and regularizing these crises. Thus to the fear, confusion, and pain inevitably attendant upon growth, we add the further burden of isolation. By labeling those voyagers who are having unusual difficulty in negotiating a standard crisis point in the identity cycle "mentally ill," we add both shame and loneliness to their struggle.

Contemporary education must provide us with new methods for constructing personal and corporate calendars and rites of passage. It must prepare us for dealing with the standard crisis points in the identity cycle and for celebrating our emergence from one stage of life to the next. Such an education would provide a map of the total life process, although the individual would still have to take the journey on his own initiative.

Since one of the most valuable functions of education is to help us understand, structure, and celebrate our times, it would seem sensible to cease thinking of schooling as an activity which is limited to the first part of life. It would make far more sense to return individuals to school at those times when they were undergoing one of the standard crises of the identity cycle. Education would then incorporate religious and moral elements as it aided us in giving birth to a vision of the integrity of the total life process. If education is concerned with wholeness it must ask: "How may we bind our times in a meaningful whole?" Church and state may remain separate, but education cannot evade the question of how we may punctuate and celebrate our time.

Finally, a course in time would have to deal with clocks and the chronological sense of time. As I was in the process of writing this chapter I slept one afternoon and dreamt that I was in a plowed field in which watches and clocks had been sown in the prepared furrows like seeds. I waited but the watches did not germinate and take root in the soil. This dream is, I think a parable of the dilemma of twentieth-century man— the organic and the fabricated are not joined, the soil and the machine form no natural ecology, the seasonal demands of life are in conflict with the imperatives of a machine-dominated economy. Measuring and fabricating, we have little patience with the slow organic processes of growth. Our machines push us. We "race" for the moon and for the electric car with anxiety lest we become victims of technology before technology can save us. And, perhaps speed kills.

The watch is a convenient symbol of the way in which machines both nurture and violate. Certainly we cannot solve the problem of the compulsive potential of machine-governed temporality by ignoring the demands of the machine. Somehow clocks and soil must grow together. *Homo faber* must learn greater wisdom, must learn to discipline his machines so that they enhance rather than destroy the psychological and natural environment necessary to a fully human life.

To date, sensitivity training has focused largely upon interpersonal relationships. We now need a new form of education in sensitivity which will make us aware of the dynamics of I-It relationships between men and machines. McLuhan has pointed out that every new technology developed has led to the atrophy of some human potential. Linear type led to the dominance of the eye and to the atrophy of the ear and the memory. The automobile, while extending our range of travel, created a generation with weak leg muscles and a high incidence of heart disease. There is nothing inevitable about this process. An educational venture which would help us to explore the need for full employment of all the senses, would provide a basis for a critique of and conversation with our machines. If we become sensitive enough to our organic rhythms and needs, there is no reason why we must allow the character of modern life to be determined by the necessity of perpetual machine-tending and consumption of what the machine produces. The time has come to talk back, to insist that clocks are made for men and not vice versa. Timeliness is more important than efficiency.

ON BECOMING A LOVER

AIM. This course will explore the various attitudes and objects of love. It will examine desire, brotherly love, friendship and gracious self-giving (*eros, philia,* and *agape*). While it will not necessarily make the student an expert in the art, it will provide him with a knowledge of alternative styles of loving and help him to remove impediments in his own personality to becoming a loving person.

RATIONALE. Love, like weather, is a perennial focus of conversation and concern. Most are aware of a drought and long for the moisture which would green-up the earth. Even though we search for happiness through power, money, knowledge, prestige, or work, most of us suspect from the beginning that of the virtues, it is love that abides. Yet we assume that love and rain fall accidentally, perhaps serendipitously, upon the just and the unjust. Love is something one falls into. By grace or luck it happens. It is not to be learned, and certainly not to be taught. Central though love is to all visions of human fulfillment, it is given no place in the curriculum.

There is one notable exception. Most love-talk quickly passes over into a discussion of the techniques and morality of the sexual act. In spite of efforts of the neo-Victorians, sex education is taking its place in the curriculum. And should it fail to receive formal status, adequate textbooks are available at any drugstore and opportunities for on-the-job training are not wanting. Unfortunately, most sex education deals largely with how babies are made, diseases avoided, or orgasms produced. And the study of the geography of the erogenous zones may make of sex a matter of genital engineering in which anxiety over performance replaces the sweet pandemonium of love. Acquiring loving habits and attitudes requires more than a study of the technology of arousal.

CONTENT AND TECHNIQUE. Carson McCullers once wrote a short story which suggests the proper place for a course in loving to begin. She tells about a young paperboy who encounters a drunk in an all-night diner. The drunk insists upon showing the boy a picture of his wife who fifteen years previously ran away with another man. He goes on to explain that in those days he did not know how to love but he has subsequently developed a science of love that will allow him to win his wife's love. The mistake he originally made was to begin with the hardest object of love—a woman. His new science establishes a hierarchy: first love a rock, then a cloud, then a tree, and gradually your powers will grow until it will be possible to love a woman. There is wisdom in this story which the Greek philosophers would have understood. Plato also insisted that love had a ladder of ascent whose lowest rung was a simple object. *Eros* is first directed toward modest objects, and only afterward may it reach the good, the beautiful, and the true. Practice in loving best begins with objects, things— rocks and trees or beautiful machines.

In order to prepare the state of mind in which erotic relatedness to objects is thinkable, some study of epistemology would be required. The relationship between knowing and loving would have to be investigated to distinguish those forms of knowledge requiring indwelling from those requiring objectifying distance. Marcel, Buber, and other existentialist philosophers have made clear the different logics of I-Thou and I-It relationships. If we are to recover an erotic relatedness to material objects, it is important to understand the difference between objects and presences, utilizing and appreciating, analyzing and contemplating, possession and cherishing, thinking about and indwelling.

Once these distinctions were understood, practice might begin in cultivating these attitudes and patterns of perception which are prerequisites of love—welcoming, wondering, and contemplating. It might be a good exercise to have students spend several weeks investigating and learning to appreciate the intricacies of a single flower or a tree. It is not difficult to predict that if such massive attention were lavished upon a single object, a new way of "knowing" and a new style of loving might emerge. Under such conditions an "it" may almost become a "thou." Erotic relatedness to things invests the natural world with a depth, a presence, a value, which is quasi-personal.

Many modern intellectuals would insist that such an experiment is doomed to fail because it is hopelessly romantic, and such a view of the natural world is no longer possible in a technological era. Romanticism is possible only in an agrarian culture. I am deeply suspicious of such objections and arguments which define in advance what it is possible to feel and believe in "the modern age." (The new criterion for authority is the concept of modernity!) Feelings are the result of the way we choose to structure our world. Hence by the choice of a life-style we decide what we will and will not see and feel. It is no less possible today to experience natural or fabricated objects with wonder and reverence than it was when the Greeks celebrated the divinity of the cosmos. Indeed, it can be argued that human survival depends upon recovering an erotic relatedness to the total environment. Love or perish! It is clear that man's alienation from and carelessness of nature must come to an end or man will destroy both himself and the world. Either we learn that we are a part of a natural ecology which must be reverenced and loved or we will not survive. Clearly alienation and pollution are two foci of the same problem. Being cut off from a natural ecology which is meaningful and sacred, man feels himself an alien, a stranger, a technological adventurer who must conquer the hostile environment of nature. Thus, in the conquest, in the search for the security which profit and capital provide, man has ruthlessly destroyed the nurturing context of nature. It is sufficient to breathe deeply on a smog-dark noon in Los Angeles, or watch oil-fouled cormorants, or see tailings from Kentucky strip mines, or birds dead from ingesting DDT to be convinced that the recovery of eros toward things is no luxury to be given low priority in curriculum development. Education must aid us in surviving, and if our hearts do not soften to love and reverence the irreplaceable heritage of earth, the waste products of our corporate greed will make the world uninhabitable.

Once students had learned to love natural and fabricated objects, the more advanced study of the nature and varieties of interpersonal love could begin. Brotherly love, friendship, or what the Greeks called *philia*, would be the first form investigated. The difference between a friend and an acquaintance is not well understood. We have come to use the word "friend" lightly, christening casual acquaintances to disguise our poverty of relationships. Much in the temperament of the modern world militates against friendship. It is not to be manufactured or produced on short notice. Nor does it thrive well in a climate where roots are constantly severed for the sake of "upward mobility." Five years (the period between moves for the *average* American family) is seeding-time for friendship. More time yet is required for the trust and fidelity which make for easy acceptance to ripen. Roots must intertwine, time be wasted together, crises weathered, celebrations shared before the relationship reaches maturity. And there is also an exclusiveness and long-range commitment involved. Intimacy requires discipline, since it may only develop where the vow of friendship has been shared. One may not be friends with everyone.

The task of exploring friendship would provide an occasion to deal with certain fundamental philosophical issues concerning the nature of time, relationship, and authentic life. In what kind of a philosophical, sociological, psychological context is friendship possible? Is it possible without covenants, promises, contracts, and vows? And if we bind ourselves to future actions and relationships, do we not thereby destroy the possibility of spontaneity? Is commitment always at the price of freedom? What is the relationship between decision, self-limitation, and freedom?

While no technique can produce friendship, the therapeutic disciplines have discovered methods for removing some of the barriers which prevent intimacy. The basic skill necessary is the ability to indwell the other with sympathetic imagination. This may be developed by communication exercises in which each member of a group must restate the cognitive and affective content of messages offered by other members. Techniques of role-playing and psychodrama are also useful in encouraging empathy and compassion. Encounter groups in which candid conversation is invited can teach the art of straight talk and help the individual to break the pattern of mixed and vague communication which prevents depth relationships from developing. If education can incorporate such techniques it can nurture empathy and create a milieu within which friendship may happen. And this is all that may be required of education.

Finally, and only finally, a course in becoming a lover should deal with genital sexuality. If the problems of genital love were placed within the context of a broader understanding of erotic relatedness and friendship, most of them would vanish. Most sexual problems are not caused by malfunctioning plumbing but by persons who have not learned how to love one another. Thus, aside from providing the necessary biological and physiological information, the major strategy I would employ in sex education would be to leave it until the end of the course. When love between man and woman happens in a relationship already rich with *eros* and *philia,* it is relieved of the pressure to be *the* validator of identity. It may then, like a chameleon, reflect whatever mood is dominant in the relationship. Lovers who are seasoned friends know that the vocabulary of flesh may be used for many things: sharing delight, fighting, binding wounds, laughing, overcoming loneliness, or affirming life when death comes near. Wisdom in loving is allowing the different seasons of love. It is not always spring.

HOW TO LOVE ENEMIES AND HATE FRIENDS

AIM. This is a course in the care, management, and resolution of conflict. It is designed to help students recognize alternative ways of dealing with aggression, anger, conflict, and competition. It will, hopefully, both decrease the level of hatred and resentment and increase the ability to enter into "loving combat" (Jaspers) with a beloved enemy.

RATIONALE. Conflict is a universal given of the human condition. Warfare is constant. Within the individual a battle goes on between perennial opponents: spirit and matter, reason and emotion, ego and id, duty and desire. Between a man and his neighbor, it is only good fences defining territorial boundaries that allow civilization its precarious victory over aggression. Among nations even the wisdom shown by territorial animals breaks down and warfare regularly leads to carnage. Corporate man has not yet learned the higher morality of the animal kingdom which ritualizes, avoids, or minimizes territorial aggression.

Yet even living in a climate of continual conflict, we are nonetheless ill-educated amateurs in the arts of battle. We are not schooled to know when it is wise to fight and when to run away (or to walk quietly with, or without, a big stick), or to distinguish creative from destructive conflict, or appropriate from mistaken targets for our anger. On the contrary, we are taught to be polite, to disguise our aggression, to keep our temper, to cover resentment with a smile to such a large extent that anger frequently emerges only in the distorted and indirect forms of masochism, sadism, or hatred which has been projected onto a unified target—The Enemy.

CONTENT AND TECHNIQUE. The place to begin is with internal conflict. Here we are immediately confronted with some fundamental questions of philosophical anthropology: Is intrapsychic warfare a defining characteristic of human nature and therefore not to be eliminated? Is man a dis-eased, a neurotic animal? Is there inevitably a conflict between essence and existence, spirit and flesh, ought and is, the idealized and the realistic self-image? Or is internal conflict a matter of cultural conditioning which we retain because we hold a philosophical view of man (Christian—idealistic—Freudian) in which a large measure of schizophrenia is accepted as inevitable? Needless to say, there are no final answers to these questions, but confronting the alternative views of the nature of the intrapsychic split in man is a fundamental part of gaining an education.

Without having to decide in advance how far inner harmony may be a desirable or an achievable goal, we may begin to explore means by which some conflicts may be resolved. The basic skill necessary is the dramatic personification of competing aspects of the personality. By identifying in turn with the bully and the coward, the judge and the judged, the victor and the victim, the child, the adult and the parent, etc., within my own personality, I come to a greater appreciation and tolerance of the multiplicity that I am. Psychodrama, inhabiting the many roles of the self, is an experiment in controlled schizophrenia. Or in democracy. All the emotions are allowed to

speak. All feelings vote. No impulse is too shameful, too forbidden, to be owned and acted out *in symbolic form.* As the
conflicting emotions and roles are dramatically inhabited, integration begins to take place. But everything depends upon
nonviolent acceptance of every aspect of the personality. The
inner forum must be democratic. Otherwise the repressed
feelings will be in constant rebellion. The many that I am
must live together. If internal censorship and repression de-
velops, one part of the personality gains a temporary victory
at the expense of the whole. When, on the other hand, forbidden emotions are recognized as a part of the self, the energy
which had been used to keep them out of awareness and to
prevent them from being acted upon is released and becomes
available for other purposes. Anger owned and symbolically
acted upon may be domesticated and turned to productive uses.

A second step in this course might be learning to deal creatively with interpersonal conflict. If students became skilled in
dramatically inhabiting the multiple aspects of their personalities, interpersonal conflict would automatically be lessened
because the need to project unacceptable feelings and judgments onto others would be minimized. However, misdirected
anger aside, there remains competition, aggression, and appropriately focused anger. The encounter group may be the best
means of educating people to fight in a creative fashion. In an
ongoing group the fight styles of the participants are seen
frequently enough to be analyzed and their creative and destructive elements understood. It is also possible to train the timid
to fight, to retrain the emotional kidney-puncher to fight
cleanly, and to help the perpetual fighter relax his defenses
long enough to receive some healing tenderness. The most
dramatic effects of fight training are with married couples.
When they learn to express feelings and differences without
equivocation, to insist upon the right to independent psychic
space, to state grievances, to demand respect, fighting may be-

come a way of loving combat. Honest fighting between friends deepens love. It is not anger but resentment, not confrontation but simmering hostility that is the enemy of love.

Finally, we come to the most difficult problem in conflict management—corporate conflict. Fighting within the self and between persons who are in emotional and physical proximity is relatively easy to humanize and make creative (in theory if not in practice). It is the warfare between remote enemies that is most bloody and destructive. When classes, races, ideologies, nations, or other corporate entities clash, little civility is shown. Dealing with this type of conflict is both the most urgent and the most baffling problem of the contemporary world. To date, education has been of little help. For the most part it has been dominated by nationalistic, ideological, religious, or class consciousness. Narrow loyalties rather than civility have shaped the curricula of the world. We have American, Russian, Chinese education, but few schools in which allegiance to the human good is viewed as the prime value to be learned.

The educational system might begin introducing the young to the history of the failures in coping with the growing horror of war. At times, reality is the only teacher. Our situation in the modern world, which is increasingly under the domination of the military mind, is perilous. The least we can do for the young is not to lie to them about the severity of the problem or to disguise our mistakes.

There are some new techniques which might aid education in going beyond corporate chauvinism. For instance, games are being developed that allow students to participate as decision-makers in simulated international, national, and local crises. Once the role of the Russian chief of defense, or the black militant has been consistently assumed in a simulation exercise, it is not quite so easy to be blind to the perspective of the stranger.

If warfare must continue, let us at least try to humanize it.

Love may never rule in the city of man, but education could
teach us that we need not kill one another in order to establish
an identity.

THE ANATOMY OF WISHING AND WILLING

AIM. This course is designed to explore and strengthen
wishing, dreaming, fantasizing, and imagining, and to demonstrate the relationship between these activities and willing and
deciding. It will provide the student with an opportunity for
learning to be at once more fanciful and more decisive.

RATIONALE. It is in vogue these days to ask how affective
elements may be introduced into the educational process. However, apart from consideration of the idea of motivation, the
conative dimension is largely neglected. Although each of us
spends a good part of the day with fantasy, dreams, and
decision-making, at no place in our educational system have
we been aided in understanding how these activities fit together.
In practice we are taught that dreams, daydreams, and fantasy
are means of escape from the real world of decision, fabrica-
tion, and action. The typical American attitude toward fantasy
is reflected in Tennessee William's play *Night of the Iguana*
where T. Lawrence Shannon suggests that the solution to the
human dilemma is to get rid of the fantastic and stick to the
realistic. Dreaming is a clandestine activity. The suspicion is
abroad that poetic, mythic, and religious languages (all forms
of organized fantasy and imagination) are subtle ways of lying
or garnishing bitter reality with sweet but illusory dreams.

Surprisingly enough we have almost as much trouble with
the notions of willing and deciding as we do with fantasy.
One would think that a culture dedicated to systems–engineering, production, and manipulation of the natural environment
would have a clear notion of the function of the will. Not true.
While appeals to will power are still made at national con-
ventions of salesmen and from pulpits serving clients who like

to believe that all problems can be solved by trying a little harder, the whole idea of autonomous willing is under a cloud. We hear little these days of the old debate: free will *versus* determinism. The silence may be due to embarrassment. So many things have combined to convince us of the impotence of willing: depth psychology has made us aware of the strangers that remain in the house of reason, the compulsion which motivates actions that are subjectively experienced as free; scientific study which isolates predictable determinants of human conduct suggests to the unsophisticated mind that all conduct is determined; the invisible economic and political powers which shape contemporary life seem to follow an automatic imperative which is insensitive to the will of individual citizens. For these and a variety of other reasons we seem to be living in a time of the eclipse of will power.

There is another factor to be considered. There is a pathology which creates the phenomenon of the mass man—*anomie* or emptiness. Where the center of life should be filled with vivid desires, animate willing, and decisive action it is a vacuum of half-hearted wishes and inconclusive acts made without internal norms. Part of the conspiracy our culture forms against fantasy also functions against desire and hope. Our "realism" warns us: "Don't hope for too much." "Tailor your desires and dreams to the possible." "The worst thing that can happen is to be disappointed, to expect too much, to desire and not be satisfied."

It may seem strange to consider fantasy, desire, and willing in the compass of a single course. However, they are so integrally related they may only be rehabilitated together. Fantasy, far from being an escape into illusion, is the way mind playfully explores alternative possibilities. Imagination allows us to try on different situations, to sample the satisfactions of different styles of life, to extrapolate the probable consequences of alternative decisions. The more fully we are conscious of dreams, daydreams, fantasies—i.e., free associations—the more likely we are to be in touch with what our total organism desires. Responsible, organic decisions can arise only when unconscious as well as conscious, playful as well as serious, sensual as well as conceptual, desires and goals are taken into account. Compulsion as well as *anomie* result when the organism is cut off from the range of possibilities which fantasy alone allows it to explore and credit. Without fantasy, novelty cannot arise. Where nothing new can be imagined the organism is driven or inhabited by the old, by visions and possibilities which were the defining limits of a former generation. Without fantasy, the fathers possess the minds of the sons and live through them. Compulsion is being possessed by a strange, an alienated will. It can be cured only when the alien will is replaced by an autonomous will which emerges when the individual ceases to repress the full range of his desired and fantastic possibilities. Potent action arises when the organism is in touch with the fullness of its desire, has explored in imagination and fantasy the probable results of alternative acts, and has taken the risk of decision and commitment to one among many possibilities.

CONTENT AND TECHNIQUES. In education dealing with the affective and the conative domains, the most important function of the teacher is to give *permission*. This is nowhere clearer than in dealing with wishing and willing. Most persons possess a wealth of dreams and fantasies which have never been cherished or taken seriously and hence have not been integrated into the total self-image. The chief function of the teacher is to give students permission to allow exiled portions of their own personalities to return home and be welcomed.

I would begin a course in wishing and willing by having students chart the geography of their dreams and fantasies. It is surprising how rapidly the unconscious responds to being taken seriously. Grant the gift of attention to dreams and they become stronger, more clearly defined, and easier to remember.

Within weeks, persons who "do not dream" discover that they can remember fragments, and then whole dreams.

Once students had recovered and shared their dreams, interpretation could begin. The fundamental rule would be: "Don't analyze! Be the dream." The symbolism of dreams is highly idiosyncratic and personal. No one is in a better position to interpret their meaning than the dreamer. The Gestalt technique of indwelling and dramatizing each item in the dream is not difficult to learn and it reveals quickly the meaning the dreamer has hidden in the symbols. For instance, if I have a dream in which an old house figures as the central symbol, I become the house and describe myself: "I am an old house. Many generations have lived in me and their marks remain. In my attic and basement you will find many strange antiques that were once useful but now are kept only for sentimental value. My basement is dark. Its floor is earthen. It smells musty. People do not like to come down to the basement often, but the furnace is there. A great deal of renovation is going on in me. Rooms are being repainted and modernized. Walls are being knocked out. Furniture is being replaced. I have even heard talk that my basement is going to be made into a game room and be brightly lighted and wood paneled, etc." It is not difficult to see how such a dream when inhabited reveals the analogy between the structure of the house and the feelings I have about my personality structure. Once this type of dramatic indwelling has taken place, other principles of dream interpretation (e.g., Freudian and Jungian) might be studied and applied.

There are numerous other techniques which might be used to strengthen the faculty of imagination. Utopias might be designed which would chart the landscape of desire for wholeness and social harmony. Guided fantasy trips could be used to explore archetypal myths and symbols. The use of analogy and metaphor might be studied. Who knows, the free association of ideas and images might lead to the rediscovery of poetry. And poetic consciousness, because it loves ambiguity and diversity and treasures playful nonsense, might provide the basis for a political critique of the deadly seriousness of a culture devoted to production, consumption, and anti-ballistic missile systems.

The second portion of this course would explore the anatomy of decision. This might be accomplished by having students analyze critical decisions they had made in the past or were yet to make. Fantasy could then be used to explore alternative pasts and futures. One of the keys to development of autonomous willing is parting with the luxury of considering oneself a victim of the past. When critical events of the past are bombarded with fantasy, alternative possibilities of response emerge. It becomes obvious that I was not merely a victim of decisions made by others. Rather, I chose, at least, my style of response. Once I take responsibility for my past I realize more clearly the measure of control I have in shaping my future. Fantasy can help me to dramatize alternative futures and thus make concrete the limits within which I may choose what I will become. Without fantasy I may never become lucid about the logic of my style of life, with its strengths and limitations, and thus may not choose with full knowledge of alternatives. Fantasy and realism are both required for lucid and virile action.

STORYTELLING AND THE DISCOVERY OF IDENTITY

AIM. This course offers the student an opportunity to write his autobiography, to experience the way in which he remembers the past, is aware of the present, and projects the future, and to reflect upon the myths and models which have influenced his life-style.

RATIONALE. Since I have written elsewhere ("Storytelling

and the Death of God," p. 82) about the function of stories in the creation of identity, I will give only a summary of the rationale for this course.

Until recent years the keystone of personal identity was participation in the shared stories, legends, and myths of a tribe, nation, cult, or church. The past, present, and future of the individual were bound together by the memories and hopes of a people to which he belonged. With the birth of secular, pluralistic, technological society, a new type of man has emerged—the man without a story, the rootless, protean man living without the stability of a tradition which he remembers with pride or a future he awaits with longing.

If the experiment of forming an ahistorical identity, living vividly in the immediacy of the present moment, seemed a human possibility, we would be led to celebrate the death of memory and hope as the event ushering in the long-desired "third age of the spirit," the paradise of spontaneity. However, at the present moment, there is much evidence (soft) which suggests that shallowness, if not illness, results from losing the depth and perspective given by memory and hope. Freud's central discovery was that neurosis is caused by repression of crucial events in our private histories, and that therapy involves making the unconscious, repressed history conscious. Since we live out of a past and toward a future, it is difficult to see how human integrity could be possible without memory or hope, without placing the present moment within a temporal context, without telling a story.

There is little immediate possibility that a new overarching myth will emerge to provide a common structure for Western man in the way the Christian myth once did. Pluralism means that we no longer have common histories or shared hopes. Therefore, if identity involves integrating past, present, and future, we must find new ways for individuals to discover and articulate their personal histories, to create their own stories.

Education must aid each student in forming the raw materials of his own experience into a coherent story.

CONTENT AND TECHNIQUE. I have had some experience in conducting workshops in which each participant explores his own story. Thus the categories and techniques which are useful for eliciting stories are somewhat clearer to me than those needed for some of the other courses I have proposed.

As in dealing with fantasy, the first step in education for storytelling is granting permission. Each of us has a story, but few have had audiences before whom it was appropriate to share intimate and meaningful history. Some, whether from wisdom or illness, have gone to professional listeners—therapists and clergymen—and have received permission to tell who they were and who they hope to become. However, our culture does not ordinarily provide a forum where the stories of individuals are shared. (The novel may be a vehicle for filling this vacuum.)

In workshops on storytelling I begin by concentrating upon the present-tense reality of participants. Often I use Zen exercises in which the mind observes the flow of thought and sensation which constitutes awareness of the present moment. The inevitable failure in this exercise makes participants aware of how difficult it is to remain in awareness without lapsing into remembering, anticipating, judging, giving explanations, having an inner dialogue (thinking) with the self, etc. A series of questions may be used to further awareness of the quality of the experience of the present: "At this point in time how do you feel about yourself and the significant people around you? What do you like, dislike, about yourself? If you were to put a motto on your sweatshirt which summarized your philosophy of life, what would it be? Complete the sentence: Happiness is . . . ."

My existentialist bias leads me to deal with the past only after the present has been considered. Memory is a function of maintaining current values, history is a tale told to illustrate a presently operative philosophy of life. In exploring the way memory preserves and creates the past, the central question the individual needs to ask is: "How did I come to be as I presently am?" There are four categories I have found particularly fruitful to investigate. What *wounds* or hurts do you resent having suffered? What *gifts* were you given for which you are grateful? Who were your important *heroes* and models? What were the crucial *decisions* for which you were responsible? These categories focus attention not only on the remembered facts which constitute the raw material of autobiography but on the way in which memory functions to justify present attitudes, such as resentment or gratitude.

We have already touched on one of the most important techniques for stimulating thought about the future—fantasy. I begin exercises in planning the future by trying to evoke the most grandiose fantasies a person entertains. If you could be, have, or do anything you wanted in your wildest daydreams, what kind of a future would you invent for yourself? After charting the outer limits of the fantastic futures which are desired, we need to introduce a note of realism. To clarify the distinction between fantasy and responsible projection, a more immediate future must be created. If everything goes perfectly for you, how will things be in ten years? What will you be doing? Feeling? What things will you have? What relationships? What will you look forward to ten years from now? Such questions dramatize the creative function of anticipating and increase potency by making clear the responsibility the individual has for creating alternatives and choosing between them. They forge the link between hope and action.

These categories, and many more which may be used to clarify present, past, and future, create an awareness of the responsibility the individual has for the way in which he invents his history. Once the integral relationship between awareness, memory, and anticipation is grasped, the unity of life style begins to emerge, and the story a person is telling with his life unfolds. Identity is discovered.

ON DYING (AND LIVING) WITH DIGNITY

AIM. Education necessarily ends with disillusionment, with the discovery that no amount of preparation or knowledge can save us from the anxiety of facing the threat and promise of the unknown, from the fear of pain, from the risk of decision, or from having to die our own death. By focusing upon death, this course will help students make the transition between the "dreaming innocence" (Tillich) of the young, in which all possibilities seem open, and the incarnate wisdom of the mature, which finds joy in accepting limits and hope in taking action.

RATIONALE. If education is to free men to change in chosen ways, it must hold up for examination the unconscious, unquestioned values, beliefs, and assumptions which pervade the life of a culture. It must deal critically with the questions and alternative life-styles which are systematically repressed. Education which fails in this prophetic task quickly degenerates into indoctrination. It fails to give distance. It is not liberating.

In the nineteenth century *the* repressed question was sex. Freud was a true educator and prophet, not because his theories about sexuality were indisputable but because he freed us from embarrassment. By lessening our shame he allowed us to claim our repressed sexuality as a treasure to be cherished. He educated by initiating us further into the reality of our bodily existence.

In the twentieth century the central repression is the awareness of death. (See *Apology for Wonder,* pp. 117 ff., for a more complete analysis.) In practice and in theory we banish death from the awareness of the living. We tranquilize the

dying, and hide them away in hospitals. And should the unthinkable happen, we turn the corpse over to strangers for
death to be disguised, by lotion to darken the skin that sun
will not warm and by lipstick to suggest that the fires of spring
still burn. In the working assumptions of our scientific quest
and in the philosophy that is emerging from the triumphant
technologist, lies the hope (curled like the serpent of illusion)
that man is immortal. The most blatant statement of this thesis
has been made by Alan Harrington:

> Death is an imposition on the human race, and no longer
> acceptable. Man has all but lost his ability to accommodate himself
> to personal extinction; he must now proceed physically to overcome
> it. In short, to kill death: to put an end to his own mortality as
> a certain consequence of being born . . . .
>
> Our new faith must accept as gospel that salvation belongs to
> medical engineering and nothing else; that man's fate depends
> first on the proper management of his technical proficiency; that
> we can only engineer our freedom from death not pray for it;
> that our only messiahs will be wearing white coats, not in asylums
> but in chemical and biological laboratories . . . . *

Surely this apocalyptic hope of "engineer[ing] our freedom
from death" is an illusion which seduces us from discovering
the realistic satisfactions of mortal existence. As Freud pointed
out, an illusion is a wish for some fulfillment which, although
logically possible, is existentially unlikely. The unattractive
middle-aged spinster who whiles away her life dreaming of
romance *might* be swept away to love and glamour by
Gregory Peck. The odds against it, however, are too high for a
reasonable wager. Hence hope invested in such wishes is mis-
placed and doomed to almost certain disappointment. Illusions
invite disillusionment. In spite of the myriad discoveries of
modern medicine, we are not one step nearer to immortality

* "The Immortalist," *Playboy,* May, 1969.

than we were in the year one. We may lengthen and make more pleasurable the span of mortality, but by no reasonable extrapolation of human knowledge or ingenuity can we hope to overcome death.

Contrary to all apocalypses, Christian, Marxist or technological, which beguile us with illusions of immortality, education must prepare men to live in a world where men are mortal, where the death of the old forms the humus out of which new life arises. Education is for humanity. Being human means returning to the soil, dying to enrich the humus.

One must choose between ancient wisdom and the apocalyptic hopes of modern technology. If the choice is made to assume that man is mortal, then we must educate men to plan wisely and joyfully in the presence of death rather than ignoring it. Classical education, particularly as seen in Platonism, Stoicism, and the religious traditions of East and West began with meditation upon death, with the conviction that until a man had faced the essential limitations of his mortality he could not develop an authentic style of life.

It is useless to pretend that we can ignore something as fundamental as death without altering our total way of experiencing the world. The immortalist has a life-style that shapes all perception, feeling, aspiration, and action. The difficult questions to consider are: In what way do hidden and/or explicit assumptions of immortality shape our perception of the world? What types of experience become difficult to negotiate because they necessitate some familiarity with death? What types of satisfactions do we barter away when we opt for the immortalist vision of man?

I would like to suggest that it is precisely those forms of ecstasy we now value most highly that become problematic when mortality is denied. It is in discovering death that joy becomes possible. Ecstasy, like love, is born in the act of dying. And he who would keep his life forever does not escape death. He only evades something of the poignancy of dying by never having known the ecstasy of being alive.

The quest for ecstasy is one way to take the sting out of death without yielding to apocalyptic illusions. Ecstasy literally means the state of being outside oneself. Such a state is accompanied by joy, enthusiasm, a sense of being a part of a moving reality that is greater than the self. We say that someone is "beside himself with joy." This is a strange metaphor. Why should the experience of being beside oneself be so intensely pleasurable? After all, most of our energies are spent in maintaining the boundaries of the ego, in constructing defense systems which will make us safe from attack by any stranger. Not surprisingly it is this success in creating a hermetic ego armed against intrusion which gives rise to the demand for ecstasy. The exaggerated individualism of Western man (with its skin-encapsulated ego) has finally produced a whole generation that has found it necessary to repeat Rimbauld's experiment of systematic derangement of the senses in the quest for ecstasy. The psychological relation between individualism and the quest for ecstasy is not hard to understand. When the self is single, when "one is one and all alone and ever more shall be so," the burden of loneliness and transcience is too great to be borne. If my identity is limited to my self, my total reality is defined by the time which lies between my birth and my death and the space through which my body travels. Solipsism is despair. The atomic self is defenseless before death. Therefore, in order to escape death and despair, a pathway beyond the self must be found, some way of getting outside the self.

The self escapes isolation and death by identification. The dying self extends its boundaries to the undying other, it invests its identity in something which abides, which is not eradicated by death. Such an escape from death is inevitably experienced as a state of rapture, ecstasy, or enthusiasm. Enthusiasm is being filled with the spirit of the deathless other.

Ecstatic identification may take many forms. The most universally sought after and convenient path is love. In love there is a mingling of identity out of which comes new life. Nature teaches us by ecstasy to plant our seed and harvest new life, to create beyond our ever-dying selves. For some there is a vocation or loyalty to a cause which expands the boundaries of the self. And there is politics. Investing the self in the community, merging private and public interests, is the source of ecstasy out of which democracy was born. Perhaps the most powerful medium of ecstasy has been mystical identification with God (alias Spirit, The All, The One, Ground of Being, etc.).

The paths to ecstasy through love, creative work, and community remain open for exploration. But the religious path is all but obscured by ideological barriers. Relativism, skepticism, positivism, radical empiricism, scientism—these are the "isms" of the toughminded which refuse man permission to transcend his atomic isolation by mysticism or metaphysics. Quite obviously, however, these "isms" have failed to exorcise the need for techniques and symbols which promote an identification with an all-inclusive totality which in other times was, without embarrassment, called God. The hallucinogenic revolution is ample evidence that the most complete ecstasy (and therefore the most complete security in the face of death) comes only with the broadest possible identification.

A lucid anticipation of death confronts us with the question of the sacred: What is it that abides? What rock is not washed away by the water? Over what does death have no dominion? What resists the acids of history? What gives the courage to conquer nihilism? What is the ultimate foundation of human dignity? To what larger than myself may I surrender? What ground (humus) nurtures my dignity? While these questions may never receive verifiable answers it is important that they be asked. At the present moment we are in great cultural confusion concerning methods of looking for answers to such religious questions. This confusion will not be easily or quickly dispelled. It seems increasingly clear, however, that since the religious need is perennial we must begin to explore new ways of doing metaphysics and cultivating the mystical experience of identification. Until we find adequate symbols to relate ourselves to our ultimate context, to identify ourselves with the mystery which encompasses us, we will remain cut off from the final ecstasy—the dignity of dying into Life.

CONTENT AND TECHNIQUE. In exploring the rationale for this course I have already suggested much of its content and technique. Its first task would be to demonstrate that a style of life is also a style of death. This could be shown by tracing the logic which joins the life- and death-styles of different models of man. We might make this study concrete by focusing upon individuals whose deaths clearly reflect different philosophies of life. For instance: Socrates, Jesus, Nietzsche, D. H. Lawrence, Freud, Bonhoeffer, Hemingway, Che Guevara, John F. Kennedy.

Following such a theoretical consideration of the integrity of life- and death-styles, it might be well to have students confront the dying. Why should we continue to banish death from our awareness, thereby isolating the dying and encouraging the growth of illusions among the living? By using the dying to teach the art of dying we might at once dispel loneliness and illusion. Exactly how educational institutions would arrange such confrontations I do not know. However, the process of working with doctors, hospitals, and agencies for the care of the terminally ill would itself be educational.

Finally, I would have each student plan his own death. In leading workshops, I have found that one of the most productive questions for encouraging individuals to assume responsibility for their own future is: How and when will you die? Many persons have death scripts which have been blindly adopted from their parents. For instance, it is not uncommon to find that if a man's father died of a heart attack

at age fifty-nine, he (the son) may operate on the semi-
conscious imperative that he also must die at or before the
age of fifty-nine in order not to become more powerful than
his father. Other persons harbor fantasies of suicide. Some
evade taking their death seriously by joking ("I plan to be
shot when I am 104 by a jealous husband").

Needless to say, the value of planning one's death is not
to ensure a coincidence between the plan and the event. How
much correlation there is between the death we plan and the death
we actually die remains an open question. Certainly the majority
of heart attacks are chosen. They are a predictable result of a
life-style which finds gratification in excessive work, alcohol,
tobacco, or food and finds little satisfaction in the active use of
the body. The important feature of planning is that it is a
way of becoming clear about the probable results of different
styles of life, in order that a lucid choice may be made. We
consider death that we might live with as much joy and integrity as possible.

As I read over the course offerings for the department of
Wonder, Wisdom, and Serendipitous Knowledge, I am aware
of how deeply they reflect the questions and concerns which
have been central to my quest. They are highly idiosyncratic.
And I am somewhat bothered by their narrowness. While I
have only my own experience upon which to reflect as a philosopher, it is obvious my story is that of a white, middle-class man
who has enjoyed the gifts of family, education, and time for reflection free from pain and poverty. The majority of clients
whom educators serve in the contemporary world do not share
this story. Thus I find myself troubled by the question: How far
may I legitimately generalize from my own experience in
establishing an educational program?

The world outside the contemporary school is vastly different
from what lay beyond the window of Mrs. Jones' classroom
in 1937. Summer warblers may still build their nests in nearby

trees but space-shots and protest demonstrations are more likely to absorb the wandering minds of students. The noise of revolution fills the air. Flux is king. Heraclitus has won the day. And what is to become of Parmenides? Is there nothing that abides? Is there no treasure education must pass from one generation to the next?

It is easy to forget what is common and perennial, to overlook the unchanging component of education. It is *persons* who are educated for maximum vividness of life. The needs, aspirations, and patterns of satisfaction of individuals differ and are shaped by race, color, creed, class, and nation. What remains the same is the need of each person to be taken seriously as one who bears a history that is nowhere duplicated, and longs for a fulfillment in life tailored to individual measurements.

Perhaps the department of Wonder, Wisdom, and Serendipitous Knowledge will offer the course listings I have suggested only as examples of the way in which one person created a curriculum to correspond to his private enthusiasms. It might then allow students to do likewise. It is not important that my summer warbler be retained in all curricula. But each person must find in the educational process something beyond learning the penmanship and grammar of his culture that gives him a name, a place, a passion, and a story.

Three

*Reflections on
a Peach-Seed
Monkey or
Storytelling and
the Death
of God*

When the great Rabbi Israel Baal Shem-Tov saw misfortune threatening the Jews it was his custom to go into a certain part of the forest to meditate. There he would light a fire, say a special prayer, and the miracle would be accomplished and the misfortune averted. Later, when his disciple, the celebrated Magid of Mezritch, had occasion, for the same reason, to intercede with heaven, he would go to the same place in the forest and say: "Master of the Universe, listen! I do not know how to light the fire, but I am still able to say the prayer," and again the miracle would be accomplished. Still later, Rabbi Moshe-Leib of Sasov, in order to save his people once more, would go into the forest and say: "I do not know how to light the fire, I do not know the prayer, but I know the place and this must be sufficient." It was sufficient and the miracle was accomplished. Then it fell to Rabbi Israel of Rizhyn to overcome misfortune. Sitting in his armchair, his head in his hands, he spoke to God: "I am unable to light the fire and I do not know the prayer; I cannot even find the place in the forest. All I can do is to tell the story, and this must be sufficient." And it was sufficient.

God made man because he loves stories.

Elie Wiesel, *The Gates of the Forest.* *

All sorrows can be borne if you put them into a story or tell a story about them . . . .   Isak Dinesen†

The first shock wave created by the recent use of the metaphor "the death of God" is beginning to subside. The religiously secure were briefly irritated because it was Christian theologians rather than atheists who were daring to use such irreverent language. But the reassurances that all was well in the world of religion began to appear. Bulletin boards in every hamlet announced sermons proclaiming, "God is *not* dead" or asking, "Is *your* God dead?" And the inevitable jokes began to be manufactured. Billy Graham is supposed to have said, "God isn't dead; I talked to him this morning." A less pious rumor circulated that God wasn't dead, only hiding in Argentina, etc. The more thoughtful members of the religious establishment took the occasion to confess the sins of the church and suggested that if only we could get on with the task of liturgical renewal, ecumenical theology, or the ministering to the social ills of the secular city, the crisis would pass. Religious language and institutions might be in need of renewal, but God remained alive and in good health.

Nor did the death-of-God theology seem to have any more profound and lasting effect upon the nonreligious community. The silent atheism of our culture, which is hidden under the pragmatic axiom which excludes all ultimate concerns from the arena of decision-making, took no notice of the supposed withdrawal of the Absolute. After all, how could such con-

---

* New York: Holt, Rinehart & Winston, 1966.
† Quoted in Hannah Arendt, *The Human Condition* (Garden City: Doubleday Anchor Book, 1958), p. 175.

siderations bear upon the practical problems of the manu-
facture of napalm or the escalating inequality between the haves
and the have-nots? And those few unorthodox but questing
persons who were conscious of the vacuum at the heart of
secularism and who were aware of living in what Koestler
described as "the age of longing" seemed as puzzled by the
solutions offered by the death-of-God theologians as the religiously pious. How confusing it was to them to find the
radical rhetoric of the death-of-God theologians compromised
by the conservative suggestion that, even if there were no
longer any God, we might, nevertheless, believe in "the fully
incarnate Word" (Altizer) or in the man, Jesus, who infected
us with the quality of "contagious freedom" (Van Buren).

Everything seems to have settled down once again, and, as
William Hamilton remarked, theologians have gone back to
the libraries, and the religious press is looking for a new story.
If no one is quite sure where we go from here, it is little
wonder. The dramatic announcement of the death of God is a
rough act to follow! With all of the drama, publicity, and
subsequent fatigue, we stand in danger of missing the real
significance of this event. Any metaphor which becomes the
darling of the mass media is likely to be overexposed and un-
derexplored. This is the fate of "the death of God," for, while
the metaphor is fast becoming a cliché, we have yet to deal
seriously with the momentous change in the self-consciousness
of Western man which gave birth to the metaphor. The crisis
in the metaphysical identity of man reflected in the metaphor
"the death of God" remains *the* unsolved philosophical and
spiritual dilemma of modern times. How we are to come to
terms with the tragic character of human existence in an age in
which there is widespread loss of confidence in all absolute
or transcendent points of reference will remain the agonizing
philosophical problem for generations after the popular press
has tired of "death-of-God" theologians.

Belief or disbelief in God involves a whole hierarchy of

ideas, attitudes, and feelings about nature, history, and the manner in which one aspires and acts within human community. Both theism and atheism are long-range, radical commitments. As Sartre has pointed out, it is not possible, without bad faith, merely to cross out the word "God" and go on existing within a theistic world of feeling and action. Thus, "the death of God" refers to a total change in the way many modern men perceive the context of their existence. The metaphysical matrix, or the spiritual ecology, of modern life is changing. The basic analogies, images, and metaphors which served to establish the metaphysical identity of traditional Western man are losing their credibility and their power to inform life.

The purpose of this essay is to explore one of the most fundamental Western metaphysical or, better, *metamundane* metaphors—the metaphor of the story. We may say that, symbolically, the identity of traditional man was based upon his ability to find his way in the forest, to light the fire, to say the prayer, and to tell a story that placed his life within an ultimate context. By the fire of sacrifice, by the practice of prayer, or by the use of some other technique of transcendence, the will of God or the gods could be determined and man could live in harmony with the powers of the overworld that exerted a mysterious influence on his existence. Each people had its own cycle of stories which located the individual within the tribe, the tribe within the cosmos, and the cosmos within the overworld. Modern man has lost his way in the forest, he cannot light the fire or say the prayer, and he is dangerously close to losing his ability to see his life as part of any story. In the bungaloid world that we are able to know with intelligence untouched by tenderness and can verify with senses which have been disciplined to exclude ecstasy, there is no transcendence. Even where the modest self-transcendence of love has remained a source of identity, there is deep suspicion that those who claim, by fire or prayer or sacred authority, to transcend the time-bound capsule in which we are all exiled are fools traffick-

ing in dreams, fantasies, and illusions. It now appears that the
ahistorical attitude created by the triumph of technological
mentality and American ideology may be destroying the function of the story as a source of metamundane identity. The
hero of the American story is Adam—the man without a
history, living in the wonderland of the innocent present.
Henry Ford stated the American dream in a manner that can
hardly be surpassed: "History is bunk." In the non-story we
tell in the new world, a man's identity is fashioned by doing
rather than remembering; his credentials for acceptance are
the skills of a trade rather than the telling of stories.

In exploring the significance of the metaphor of the story,
I will suggest that telling stories is functionally equivalent to
belief in God, and, therefore, "the death of God" is best
understood as modern man's inability to believe that human
life is rendered ultimately meaningful by being incorporated
into a story. After exploring the history of storytelling and of
the metaphor of the happening which is the contemporary
candidate to replace the story as the clue to the ultimate context
of human existence, I shall try to rehabilitate the story as a
basic tool for the formation of identity. This is where the peach-
seed monkey comes in. I will try to find out from him whether
theology may find a new method for telling stories and for
locating the presence of the holy in a time when the orthodox
stories about the "mighty acts of God" no longer inform
Western identity.

I | A Short History of Storytelling

The significance of the story in archaic or preliterate cultures
is well illustrated in a remark Laurens Van Der Post made
about the Kalahari Bushmen:

The supreme expression of his spirit was in his stories. He was a wonderful storyteller. The story was his most sacred possession. These people knew what we do not: that without a story you have not got a nation, or a culture, or a civilization. Without a story of your own to live you haven't got a life of your own. *

Preliterate man lived in a world which received its intellectual, religious, and social structure through the story. Each tribe had its own set of tales, myths, and legends which defined the metaphysical context within which it lived, gave a history of the sacred foundation of its social rituals, and provided concrete models of authentic life. Membership in the tribe involved retelling and acting out the shared stories which had been passed on from generation to generation since the beginning of time. As the studies of Eliade show, archaic man sought to avoid the profane and to live in the realm of the sacred. Sacred acts were those which could be traced back to some archetype which had been originated by a god or hero. Thus, the telling of stories was a way of justifying and sanctioning those values which were essential to the preservation of the community. Wealth and status were often measured in archaic societies more by the stories a man knew, the rituals he was authorized to conduct, and the dances he could perform than by the cattle and possessions he had accumulated. The story served the diverse functions of philosophy, theology, history, ethics, and entertainment. It served to locate the individual within the concentric circles of the cosmos, nature, the community, and the family, and it provided a concrete account of what was expected of a man and what he might expect in that darkness which lies beyond death.

The centrality of storytelling in the formation of the identity and culture of preliterate man is well established, although it remains somewhat embarrassing to modern man. Since the enlightenment and the emergence of less dramatic but more

* *Patterns of Renewal* (Wallingford, Penn.: Pendle Hall Pamphlets, 1962), p. 9.

scientific modes of thought, Western man has found great comfort in telling himself that he has come of age and passed beyond the primitive darkness of myth into the full light of reason. Therefore, in most accounts of the intellectual history of man, one may detect a sigh of relief when the narrative leaves the poetic-mythical thought of archaic man and focuses on the development of rational philosophical thought in the Greek city-state. The march toward the sun has begun! The education of the human race toward a world in which we no longer need to tell stories has progressed a step.

Unfortunately, this picture is more myth than fact. Although empirical science and philosophical reason had faint beginnings in classical Greece, the fundamental philosophical vision which animated Greek life was as solidly dramatic and mythological as that of archaic man.

Something of the Greek's estimate of the significance of storytelling may be gleaned from Hannah Arendt's suggestion that, symbolically, the *polis* was created by the heroes coming home from the Trojan Wars, who wanted an arena in which their deeds might be recounted and remembered. Democracy sprang from the need for an audience which would continue to applaud a hero after his death. Immortality was being included in a story which would be retold. Thus, the ultimate measure of a man was lost if his life was not lived in such a way that his deeds would fit into a broader story which future generations would preserve. Politics was to make the world safe for storytelling and, thus, for immortality.

The metaphor of the story goes even deeper into Greek thought. For the Greek mind, no less than the primitive, the key analogy by which human existence was interpreted was the seasonal rhythm of nature. The yearly vegetation cycle was a drama which provided the clue to the identity of the human soul. It was Dionysus, a god of vegetation, who gave birth to theatre. The soul, the cosmos, and the drama share a common structure:

Act One. Spring: Innocence, vitality, and promise. In the first green of life (which is gold), there is an announcement of intention. Birth contains a hidden promise of fulfillment; in the beginning is the end (the *telos*). The acorn promises the oak; the child, the man; potentiality looks forward to actuality. All life in its inception bears within it the promise of perfection. Thus, in the beginning there is no death. In childhood the promise of life is so overwhelming that knowledge of death is absent. Life begins with innocent immortality and humble omnipotence.

Act Two. Summer and Fall: Maturation and disillusionment. In actuality the promise is only partially fulfilled. The acorn grows into a stunted oak, and not every child matures into the essential humanity of a Socrates. By late summer it becomes obvious that maturation is always tragic, and the promise given in the beginning is doomed to be broken. The mature plant does not achieve the status of the ideal, and man is forever exiled from the perfection for which he longs. As summer passes into fall or as the verdant suppleness of life gives way to the brown brittleness of incipient decay, hope becomes strained, and the promise of life is transformed into the anxious question: The greenness of life is passing; will it ever return?

Act Three. Winter: Death and despair. Winter is always a crisis, both to the body and to the spirit. The disappearance of the vegetation raises to consciousness the suspicion and the lurking fear that the promise given in springtime was an illusion. Does not winter, perhaps, signify that life is ebbing away, that darkness triumphs over light, and that death has final dominion over life?

Act Four. Spring: Resurrection and return. Rebirth, although perennial, always comes as a surprise and a gift. As the sun gathers strength and impregnates the earth with the promise of green, the anxiety of winter is replaced by hope and the cosmos is reborn out of chaos.

It was this drama which was the structural warp upon which

the diverse modes of Greek experience were woven. We find this same story celebrated in the myths of the simple and the philosophies of the sophisticated. For the literal-minded there were the stories of the vegetation deities, such as Demeter, who lived half of the year in the underworld and the other half among mortals, or Dionysus, who was god of both ecstasy and death. For the intellectuals who had lost faith in the old myths there was the demythologized philosophy of Plato, which offered arguments to show the unity and immortality of the cosmos and the soul, or the more astringent philosophy of Aristotle, which presented the whole cosmos as a hierarchy of interrelated substances, all driven by the desire to actualize the potentiality with which they were pregnant. In Socrates the Greek world also had its incarnation of the vision of the man who knew his soul was as immortal as the cosmos. The ethics of Plato, Aristotle, and the Stoics are little more than theoretical commentaries on the type of life exemplified in Socrates. In the story of the death of Socrates it becomes clear why his biography could serve as the summary and ethical focus of the Greek vision of life. As the poison reaches his vital organs, Socrates lifts his head and says, "Crito, I owe a cock to Asclepius. Will you remember to pay the debt?" Strange and courageous words these are for a dying man! At the onset of death Socrates remembers he owes a debt to the god of healing. By this act he confesses his confidence in the dramatic unity of life and death and his belief that the promise of immortality which informs the soul is destined for fulfillment. Thus, the cosmic drama of life comes to be exemplified in a biography which became as normative for the Greek mind as the biography of Jesus was later to become for the Christian community.

In the Judeo-Christian tradition the drama which provides the structural meaning for human existence takes place on the stage of history rather than in the eternal cycle of nature. The whole of history is a story for which God has provided the script. Unlike the endlessly recurring drama of seasonal life, the story being told in history is once told; each moment is unique, even though it fits into the development of the plot. The drama of history may be summarized thusly:

Prelude. The Judeo-Christian story begins with the Story-teller—"In the beginning, God . . . ." The stage upon which the drama of history is played out is not eternal. Man and the cosmos had their beginning in the creative intention of a transcendent God. Thus, the stage and the actors are created for the drama. Why God chose to create the drama of history remains a mystery. Perhaps he was lonely and wanted to share his love. Or, as Wiesel suggests, it may be that he loved stories. At any rate, the reason is unimportant, or at least unknowable, and all man needs to know to orient himself in history is the outline of the drama which is being developed.

Act One. In the Garden. Like most good stories which undertake to explain human existence, this one begins its account of man with a picture of the innocence and harmony which ruled life in the mythical era of "once upon a time" (an era which is always present in the depth of the psyche). In the Garden of Eden there is finitude but no tragedy. In its ontological depths, life is good and has within itself the resources for its own fulfillment. In spite of the limitations which are represented by sexuality and the inevitability of death, there is no shame or estrangement in essential, or created, human life. The movement of life against death, the spirit against the flesh, or the id against the ego, which plays so large a part in the development of history, is alien to the intention of the Story-teller.

Act Two. The Fall. The biblical tradition does not explain the fall; it only describes it. Why history involves the tragic rupture of harmony between man and his environment (social, natural, and ultimate) remains a mystery. The story of Adam and the forbidden fruit merely illustrates the mystery of evil which is a part of the problem of historical human existence. The fall represents the moment when the story begins to develop in a manner not intended by the Storyteller. God experiences what every author does: having created a character to tell a story, he finds the character rebelling against the intention of the author and insisting upon telling his own story. Historical existence (the time lying between "once upon a time" and "someday") is the time of conflicting themes during which the Storyteller is forced to improvise, making use of the dialogue and action created by his recalcitrant characters, to salvage the story he intended to tell. His control over the development of the drama is real but tenuous as the agents of the snake, for the moment, remain powerful enough to destroy the intended artistic unity of the story. However, to those who have ears to hear, there is a promise hidden in the confused tale of history: the Storyteller will regain control of his creation and bring it to its intended fulfillment. There are the signs of the rainbow, the pillar of fire and the cloud of smoke, the old covenant sealed with commandments written in stone, and the new covenant which is written on the flesh. But here we are getting ahead of the story.

Act Three. In the End. Someday alienation will come to an end, and the story of history will reach the conclusion for which it is destined. In the end, as in the beginning, the intent of the Storyteller will be made manifest; the promises and possibilities with which history was pregnant in the Garden of Eden are brought to full birth in the kingdom of God. Judaism and Christianity have a fundamental disagreement about when the "sometime" is when history will reach its conclusion. For Christianity, spring has already begun in the cold midwinter of history; in the life, death, and resurrection of Jesus, the new era has its beginning. From this beginning it will grow rapidly, like a mustard seed, blotting out the estrangement and tragedy which have ruled history. For Judaism, the kingdom of God, which is both the *finis* and the *telos* of history, still lies in the future. The messiah, the herald of the end, has not yet come, but perhaps "next year in Jerusalem . . . ."

The different acts of the drama of history reflect also the movement of the life of the individual. Each man is Adam, bearing within himself a nostalgia for perfection which is a silent testimony that he is an exiled citizen of a country in which there is no estrangement. As Augustine stated the matter, "Thou hast made us for thyself, O God, and our hearts are restless till they rest in Thee." Thus, each individual repeats within himself the pilgrimage of history. As a wayfarer, man (*Homo viator*) is never totally lost, because he knows the story of the garden from which he came and the kingdom toward which he travels. If exile is difficult to bear, there is, at least, the comfort of the promise of homecoming; there is hope which is "a memory of the future" (Marcel). And for the Christian, there is, in the figure of Jesus, a biography which is revelatory of the ultimate intention of the creator of history which also provides a model for the conduct of life. For the pilgrim, authentic life lies in the imitation of Christ. Like the archaic man, both Jew and Christian belonged to a community in which the identity of the individual was shaped by shared stories and common models.

In a certain sense, we may date the birth of the modern world at the point when the Judeo-Christian story ceased to entertain and fascinate and new stories and ideologies were created which reflected man's growing love affair with the earth. Although the new stories no longer spoke of the gods or of God, the outline of the drama which Greek and Christian shared was still not changed. The costumes and the language changed, but the plot remained the same. In the new languages of politics, economics, philosophy, technology, and psychology, the drama of innocence/fall/recovery-of-innocence was retold. The enlightenment tried to replace the period of original innocence with the notion of the gradual education of the human race from the darkness of mytho-poetic thought into the full light of reason, but innocence returned in romanticism, social-ism, and the ideology of American democracy. Once again, the various gospels proclaimed that man was born free, had fallen into chains, and was shortly to enter into a new birth of free-dom. In romanticism the noble savage fell from nature into repressive civilization, but the redemption of spontaneity was shortly to be ushered in by poetry, or free love, or psycho-analysis. In socialism and communism the fall was from civility into class struggle, but the era of redemption, in a classless society without exploitation or alienation, was shortly to arrive by the inevitable logic of history and the devotion of the elect. In the ideology of American democracy, the inalien-able rights of man had been compromised by adherents of monarchy and tradition but were soon to be restored and rendered safe by the emergence of a new nation which would make the world safe for democracy. On American soil Adam became the hero once again.

It is only within the present century that the metaphor of the story and the outline of the traditional drama which have been commonplace in Western civilization have been radically criticized and widely abandoned. For the contemporary intel-lectual the metaphysical myth has ceased to provide the context for identity. The conviction is gone that history tells a story or that reality may be appropriately known in dramatic terms. While we retain and share such political myths as those clus-tering around the labels "democracy" and "communism," we have lost the metamundane myths and even the confidence in their possible usefulness.

The new metaphor which reflects modern experience is *the happening*. Nature and history are governed by chance and probability. Luck is the only god, and crossing the fingers or knocking on wood is the only liturgy appropriate to a happen-stance world. One thing happens after another, and, although there are causes for events, there are no reasons. Nowhere in nature or history does the modern intellectual find evidence of a guiding mind which gives coherence to what is still, erroneously, called the uni-verse. If history tells a tale, it is the tale of the idiot. It is up to the individual to give his own life meaning by creating a project to which he may give himself.

Antoine Roquentin, the hero of Sartre's novel *Nausea*, presents a vivid example of the man who has become a victim in a world where things just happen. He confesses that he always wanted to be able to see his own life develop with the form and symmetry of a character in a novel. It is precisely this demand which leads to his disillusionment.

> This is what fools people: a man is always a teller of tales, he lives surrounded by his stories and the stories of others, he sees everything that happens to him through them; and he tries to live his own life as if he were telling a story. *

In real life there are no beginnings or endings; there are no moments of intrinsic significance which form a framework of meaning around experience. There are only days "tacked on to days without rhyme or reason, an interminable, monotonous addition."** The refrain that runs throughout *Nausea* is "anything can happen"; no universal reason sets limits to the possible and gives meaning to human history. In the face of the absurdity of existence, the only option for the lucid individual is to create a reason for existing by writing a book or joining a political movement, etc. Only by choosing some project, however arbitrary, can the individual fill the present moment and escape the nausea which results from awareness of the absolute contingency and absurdity of existence.

The existentialist hero who tries to live in the immediacy of the present moment is a figure who typifies our age. He is the stranger in Camus's novel, the beatnik of a generation ago

---

* Jean-Paul Sartre, *Nausea* (New York: New Directions Books, 1959), p. 56.
** *Ibid.*, p. 57.

who turned up in Kerouac's *On the Road,* and, most recently, he is the hippy who opts out of traditional culture and tunes in on the vibrations. Wherever he appears, one metaphysical assumption governs identity—there is no future, there is no past, so live in the moment. Marshall McLuhan tells us that this world of happenings, of "all-at-once-ness," is a product of the media. The linear, historical, storytelling mentality belonged to another age. In the tribal village of the electronic world no framework or perspective is possible—only total immersion. The perspective of the past, which has sometimes been called the wisdom of our fathers, is of no use to the existentialist hero. Indeed, anyone over thirty (unless he can sit in the lotus position) is already relegated to the scrapheap of the past.

The world defined as happening is merely the world from which God has departed. Over a century ago Dostoevski reduced the functional significance of the absence of God to one sentence: if God is dead, all things are possible. The concentration camps and the systematic use of what Marcel called "techniques of degradation" have demonstrated that all things are morally possible; the will-to-power makes it possible to violate all that past generations have considered sacred. As Richard Rubenstein has shown in *After Auschwitz,* the destruction of all moral limits roots in the desire to kill God and be rid of all restraint to pleasure. The metaphysical vision of a completely contingent world in which "anything can happen" has been explored by Sartre and by the Theater of the Absurd. Where chance is considered the ultimate metaphysical category, the world is reduced to radical pluralism, discontinuity, and chaos. If there is no overarching principle of order or meaning, the order—moral and physical—which we have observed in the past cannot be projected into the future. Lacking any metamundane principle of unity, we can have no assurance of any continuity between past and future; thus, remembering and planning are equally futile. Spontaneity has replaced storytelling as the mode of authentic life.

By looking at the function the story served in traditional cultures and by contrasting the situation of the contemporary intellectual living in a happenstance world, we can get some notion of the implicit confession of faith involved in the act of telling a story and some measure of what has been lost.

In telling stories, traditional man was affirming the unity of reality. The individual, the tribe, nature, and the cosmos fit together in concentric circles of integrated meaning. All of the parts were necessary to form a coherent and artistic whole. Past, present, and future were, likewise, bound together in a thematic unity. Thus, the individual standing on the ever-disappearing point of present time could affirm that the meaning of his existence was not destroyed by the passing of time. He took courage from his knowledge that he had roots in what had been and that his memory and deeds would be preserved in what would be. In effect, the story affirmed that the reality of the individual was not reducible to the present moment of experience but belonged to a continuity of meaning that the flow of time could not erode. With this faith the individual could act with a sense of continuity and perspective; his spontaneity was tempered by memory and hope.

Another article of faith hidden in the act of storytelling is the confidence that the scale of Being is such that a human being can grasp the meaning of the whole. Personality is not an epiphenomenon in an alien world of matter ruled by chance and number but is the key to the cosmos. Man is a microcosm; thus, in telling his stories, he may have confidence that his warm, concrete, dramatic images are not unrelated to the forces that make for the unity of the macrocosm. While his images and stories may reduce the proportions of reality to a scale that is manageable by the human spirit, their distortion serves the cause of truth. Traditional man had every confidence that his symbols, myths, and stories were the most appropriate means to grasp reality and were not merely illusions projected out of his isolated, subjective brain.

It is too soon to evaluate the success of the modern effort to get along without the belief that history tells a story or that there is a meaningful continuity between past, present, and future. Whether a viable and creative identity can be formed where the ultimate symbol is the happening is questionable. Our knowledge of the dynamics of personality would suggest that it is psychologically impossible to attain the goal of spontaneous action except by an integration of all the modes of temporal experience. Genuine spontaneity is possible only to the person who has accepted the limits imposed upon him by his past experience and who is animated by some meaning he seeks to realize in his future. Gratuitous action is a parody of spontaneity in which unconscious motives drive a person to act in a manner totally discontinuous with his past. It is at least dubious whether any mature form of personality integration is conceivable in which the individual has not come to accept and relish his past and integrate it with his projects for the future. Nietzsche remarked that a man must come to love his wounds. To do this he must be able to weave his past and his hopes for the future into one coherent story. However this may be, without prejudging the modern experiment of forming an identity in the context of absurdity and discontinuity, we may ask a more modest question. Recognizing that the metaphor of the happening expresses the spiritual atmosphere of the contemporary world, we may ask whether we are forced to capitulate to this climate or whether it is permissible to change it. Are we condemned to live in a chaotic world of the happening with the view that our past is insignificant and our future non-existent? Is there any intellectually respectable alternative to the view that God is dead and every man must give meaning to his personal existence? Is identity with continuity possible? Can there be any theology after the death of God or any account of a principle of metamundane unity and meaning operative in history?

II | *A Way beyond the Death of God— or How to Tell Stories*

We must begin our search with the realization that no form of neo-orthodoxy provides a viable starting point. The orthodox metamundane myths of religion are no longer supported by any authority strong enough to command the respect of an unprejudiced inquirer. Knowledge of comparative religions, textual criticism, and the dynamics of symbol formation and functioning has destroyed our ability to grant a priori authority to any religious tradition. For the moment, at least, we must put all orthodox stories in brackets and suspend whatever remains of our belief-ful attitude. Our starting point must be individual biography and history. If I am to discover the holy, it must be in *my* biography and not in the history of Israel. If there is a principle which gives unity and meaning to history it must be something I touch, feel, and experience. Our starting point must be radical.

We may use a series of questions to suggest a method which may lead us back to storytelling and theology. Is there anything on the native ground of my own experience—my biography, my history—which testifies to the reality of the holy? Since the word "holy" in this question is, itself, problematic, we may further translate it into functional terms. Thus, to restate our first question in operational terms: Is there anything in my experience which gives it unity, depth, density, dignity, meaning, and value—which makes graceful freedom possible? If we can discover such a principle at the foundation of personal identity, we have every right to use the ancient language of the holy, and, therefore, to mark out a domain for theological exploration.

Since I have shifted the ground of theology to the individual and the quotidian, I can proceed only by telling my story and then by inviting my reader to tell his.

Once upon a time when there were still Indians, Gypsies, bears, and bad men in the woods of Tennessee where I played and, more important still, there was no death, a promise was made to me. One endless summer afternoon my father sat in the eternal shade of a peach tree, carving on a seed he had picked up. With increasing excitement and covetousness I watched while, using a skill common to all omnipotent creators, he fashioned a small monkey out of the seed. All of my vagrant wishes and desires disciplined themselves and came to focus on that peach-seed monkey. If only I could have it, I would possess a treasure which could not be matched in the whole cosmopolitan town of Maryville! What status, what identity, I would achieve by owning such a curio! Finally I marshaled my nerve and asked if I might have the monkey when it was finished (on the sixth day of creation). My father replied, "This one is for your mother, but I will carve you one someday."

Days passed, and then weeks and, finally, years, and the someday on which I was to receive the monkey did not arrive. In truth, I forgot all about the peach-seed monkey. Life in the ambience of my father was exciting, secure, and colorful. He did all of those things for his children a father can do, not the least of which was merely delighting in their existence. One of the lasting tokens I retained of the measure of his dignity and courage was the manner in which, with emphysema sapping his energy and eroding his future, he continued to wonder, to struggle, and to grow.

In the pure air and dry heat of an Arizona afternoon on the summer before the death of God, my father and I sat under a juniper tree. I listened as he wrestled with the task of taking the measure of his success and failure in life. There came a moment of silence that cried out for testimony. Suddenly I remembered the peach-seed monkey, and I heard the right words coming from myself to fill the silence: "In all that is important you have never failed me. With one exception, you kept the promises you made to me—you never carved me that peach-seed monkey."

Not long after this conversation I received a small package in the mail. In it was a peach-seed monkey and a note which said: "Here is the monkey I promised you. You will notice that I broke one leg and had to repair it with glue. I am sorry I didn't have time to carve a perfect one."

Two weeks later my father died. He died only at the end of his life.

For me, a peach-seed monkey has become a symbol of all the promises which were made to me and the energy and care which nourished and created me as a human being. And, even more fundamentally, it is a symbol of that which is the foundation of all human personality and dignity. Each of us is redeemed from shallow and hostile life only by the sacrificial love and civility which we have gratuitously received. As Erik Erikson has pointed out in *Identity and the Life Cycle,* a secure and healthy identity is founded upon a sense of *basic trust* which is first mediated to a child by the trustworthiness of his parents. Identity has its roots in the dependability, orderliness, and nurturing responsiveness of the world of primal experience. That civility which separates men from the lower animals depends upon the making and keeping of promises, covenants, vows, and contracts. As Nietzsche so aptly put the matter, man is that animal who makes promises.

When I uncover the promises made and kept which are the hidden root of my sense of the basic trustworthiness of the world and my consequent freedom to commit myself to action, I discover my links with the past; I find the "once upon a time" which is the beginning of the story I must tell to be myself.

In the same act of recovering the principle of my identity, I discover a task for my future; being the recipient of promises, I become the maker of promises. I seek to manifest that same faithfulness toward others which was gratuitously shown to me. In identifying myself as one who lives by promises and promising, I find the principle which gives unity to my life and binds together the past, the future, and the present. Without losing the spontaneity of significant action in the present, I transcend every dying moment toward my roots in the past and my end in the future. I have a story.

A series of questions arises at this point. Is the peach-seed monkey not of mere individual significance? While it may be of symbolic significance in the biography of Sam Keen, does it not lack the universal element which allowed the metamundane myths of former generation to be the shared property of a community? Does the intimate character of such a story merely point to the dilemma of the twentieth-century man, whose biography is not inserted into any shared mythological structure? And, finally, how can such a story lay claim to a theological meaning?

Two major discoveries of Freud may help us to see the universal dimension of what initially appears to be merely an incident in an individual biography.

First, the psychoanalytic method is based upon the assumption that each man has repressed crucial pages of his own history because they are too painful to remember. The path to health involves the de-repression of these hidden memories and the reconstruction of the individual's personal history. The implication of psychoanalytic theory is clear: the crucial history the individual must recover to be whole is familial rather than communal. Each individual must search out both the fidelities and the infidelities and both the wounds and the gifts which gave the unique character to his biography.

Second, although the Freudian path to salvation begins with the isolated individual's learning to tell his own story, it does not end here. Freud's second great discovery (which we usually associate with the name of Jung) was that once the individual recovers his own history, he finds it is the story of every man. For example, when shame and fear dissolve and I am able to confess that I hated as well as loved (or vice versa) the father who nurtured me, I discover that I am one with Oedipus. It is only a step from this insight to the realization that hating the father and rebelling against God are inseparable. Thus, being Oedipus, I am also Adam and Prometheus and all of the heroes and antiheroes of history. The more I know of myself, the more I recognize that nothing human is foreign to me. In the depth of each man's biography lies the story of all men.

The peach-seed monkey, thus, belongs as much to you as to me. Who can deny that his civility and humanity have been nurtured by a matrix of promise too rich and intricate to detail? To be minimally human involves the use of language and reason which can only be learned where there has been a modicum of civility and promise-keeping. He who reads or speaks confesses in that very act he has been succored, educated, and humanized in a social matrix. Psychological reflection shows that when the individual goes to the heart of his own biography unhampered by shame or repression, he finds there a universality of experience that binds him to all men.

If we look more deeply at the story of the peach-seed monkey, we discover that it has a theological as well as a universal significance. There is, of course, no way in which the existence, activity, or reality of God can be demonstrated from such a story. Therefore, if the criterion for theological significance is the use of God-language, the matter ends here. As we suggested earlier, however, theological language need not be limited to God-talk. Any language is authentically theological which points to what is experienced as holy and sacred. And we may now define the holy as "that irreducible principle, power, or presence which is the source and guarantor of unity, dignity, meaning, value, and wholeness." If such a phenomenological and functional definition of theological language is permissible, it becomes obvious that the peach-seed monkey points to a dimension of reality which is sacred. The sanctity of promises is the *sine qua non* of humanness; it is the principle upon which identity and community are founded.

Traditional theists and humanists alike will deny that any principle grounded in purely human commitment is a candidate for theological honors. Both will maintain that theology has to do with the extraordinary rather than the ordinary, the supernatural rather than the natural, or the transcendent source rather than the subterranean foundations of life. A phenomenological approach does not allow us the luxury of such a segregation of the holy. If we begin with a description of the functional significance of the encounter with the holy, we are forced to conclude that the power to give unity and meaning to life which was once mediated by metamundane myths is today experienced as present in the principles which are the foundation of identity and community.

By locating the holy in the spiritual depths rather than the heights—in the quotidian rather than the supernatural—the form and imagery, not the substance, of the religious consciousness is changed. If the promises that redeem us spring from mundane soil rather than from an authorized covenant with God, history is, nevertheless, experienced as the story of promise and fulfillment. Human existence is still sanctified by sacrifice, and we may appropriately face the mysterious givenness of life and personality with gratitude and reverence. This change in language from images of height to depth represents the religious response of the twentieth-century mind to the loss of the traditional metamundane myths. If God is gone from the sky, he must be found in the earth. Theology must concern itself not only with the Wholly Other God but with the sacred "Ground of Being" (Tillich)—not with a unique incarnation in past history but with the principles, powers, and persons which are presently operative to make and keep human life luminous and sacred.

Whether such a subterranean theology will allow us to weather the crisis in spiritual identity through which we are passing is still unknown. For those who no longer find in the stories and myths of orthodox religion the power to inform life with creative meaning, it may, at least, point to a locality and a method which may be useful in discovering a sacred dimension of life. And, perhaps, if each of us learns to tell his own story, even if we remain ignorant of the name of God or the form of religion, it will be sufficient.

Four

*Diary
of a
Jubilee Year*

Most books in philosophy or theology give a distorted picture of the nature of thinking. Since they reach the public only in polished form, the illusion is created that philosophical thinking is linear, formal, and finds its way without hesitation from problems to solutions. The actual process of philosophical thought is more like making repeated forays into an unexplored country. With each journey the details of the landscape become more evident and a rough-scale map begins to emerge. Clarity is gained gradually at the cost of enduring turmoil. If a philosopher is seriously concerned to deal with the tensions, ambiguities, and tragic dilemmas he faces as an existing human being, the clarity of his thought will be in direct proportion to his courage in tolerating the anxiety involved in gaining new knowledge. Tillich once remarked that all new knowledge involves anxiety and guilt. To eat of the fruit of the tree of the knowledge of good and evil is to incur the wrath of the gods, or at least to challenge the dictates of the superego.

I thought it only fair that the reader be taken behind the scenes and be given a glimpse of the process out of which these essays grew. This account is neither strictly philosophical nor biographical. It is something of both. It records many of the conversations that take place between the voting members of the commonwealth that is Sam Keen. I am convinced that it is necessary for every citizen to be allowed to say his piece. Thus, there will be voices that shout in anger, others that plead, some that are defiant. The lost and the hostile will be heard as well as the grateful and the joyful. No doubt, all are not allowed to speak. No government refrains from repressing some of its citizens when they appear too seditious. I do not applaud such repression, but only recognize it. There are voices within me I would like to banish in order to keep the peace. But I have tried to be as democratic as I currently have the courage to be, since I am convinced that lucidity, power, and joy are most fully present where there is the least repression.

After a particularly delightful party given by a publisher for a group of radical theologians (held in a Yugoslav restaurant with sweet wine, strong music, and a permissive attitude toward dancing), I was given a button which read:

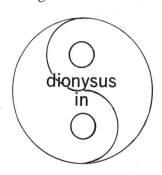

If I could assign a title to the central theme of my experience during this year it would be taken from this button given me shortly before I left Louisville to spend a sabbatical year in California investigating the "human potential" movement. It has, indeed, been Dionysus in 1969. It has been a year to explore the limits and boundaries I previously defined for myself, a year for the expansion of consciousness, a year for sampling novelty, a year for dancing. There are citizens who fear the dance, who want to keep things as they were. Thus conversation has sometimes been lively and heated. Writing this diary has helped me to clarify the issues and keep the dialogue from breaking down.

UNDATED.

SILENCE

In the beginning was silence.
Before the word was chaos.
And night.

Then spirit moved across the waters.
A word came forth.
Meaning was given to form, direction to motion, order to chaos.
A world emerged.
The word bore one in its own likeness.

Words went forth and covered the earth, giving and destroying.
There was greatness and tragedy in names
Until the word-bearer grew tired and speechless.
History grew stale and cluttered with noise.
And the silent stars told no story.
In the fullness of silence time grew pregnant.
A word was born from chaos.
There was light and life
A new heaven and a new earth
And healing in speech.

And the word became words, and words, and words, and words,
        and words, and words,
And there was silence and chaos.
And out of the silence came . . . ?

AUGUST 15, 1968. ECSTASY AND POLITICS

One of the crucial questions: "To what may I give myself?"
If I do not ask it with seriousness I end up, at best, a lonely
man "fulfilling my potential," concentrating on myself. At
worst I descend into despair. The questions of surrender, belonging, self-transcendence, loyalty, ecstasy must be asked.
Otherwise I possess myself like a jealously guarded territory.
I watch over my boundaries, possessions, energies. I hoard
myself. I become a territorial animal.

If I belong to nobody, no corporation, there is no ecstasy.
Ecstasy is when bodies meet and boundaries are overcome, in
sex and politics. Love's body is not word-play (Norman Brown
is wrong), but politics. Caring must be made concrete, otherwise there is no incarnation, no fleshing-out of love. Incarnation is incorporation. Organization is the embodiment of love.
Transcending self by entering into another body (physical or
political) is ecstasy. Love and politics are the alternatives to
the lonely self-transcendence of drugs. Stay in the body or you
become nobody. Incorporate or die. Incarnate or turn-on, tune-
in, and cop-out.

OCTOBER 8, 1968. DIALOGUE WITH FEAR

SK: *I wish I could begin by saying, "Damn you, fear. Leave
me alone!" but honesty demands that I address you as "Dear
fear," for you have been with me most of my life. Now I want
to understand why I am attracted to you and did not banish
you long ago.*

FEAR: *I am glad you are willing to admit that we are reluctant
friends. It has taken me some years to get you to confess that
you are a hesitant lover of what you pretend to despise. What a*

capacity for self-deceit you have, pretending that I was some-how your fated enemy! Or, to be specific, that I was an un-conscious legacy from your parents. Such transparent nonsense. If I am your fate, I am at least a fate you have chosen and nurtured. It is not without your consent and satisfaction that we have been together all these years. You might have lived in conversation with love, or courage, or creativity, or desire, or fame. No! You have kept me around. So don't try to disown me.

SK: *O.K. you have me. I admit some responsibility for con-tinually talking with you but I certainly do not get satisfaction from your presence. You are like a bad neighbor. I am stuck with you but I wish you would move away.*

FEAR: *You lie easily. The fact is I am a valuable companion and a loyal friend. I don't demand change of you. I am satis-fied to keep our relation as it has always been. I do not ask you to venture out into the unknown or act heroically in de-fining your existence in the carelessness and caprice of the world. All I ask is a token, a ritual, a guarantee that you will not go beyond the limits I have set for your comfort and safety.*

SK: *Ritual or token, hell! You demand the most alive part of me. Your "token" is the whole of my capacity for new experi-ence. You promise security so long as I surrender my autonomy, my critical ability, my reason, my responsibility for reflecting upon and evaluating my own experience. Your price for com-fort is giving up growth.*

FEAR: *So what if the price is high? If you refuse to acknowl-edge my authority you will fall into pride and rebellion. I keep the boundaries. I set the limits. Only Adam, Prometheus, and other proud but foolish rebels have the illusion that they are strong enough to define the nature of good and evil for them-selves. No man, and least of all you, has the wisdom, the energy, or the time to determine the limits of the possible for himself. Such omnipotent pretense is clearly sinful and stupid.*

SK: *You sound so reasonable and charitable. But, in truth, you wear the face of the Grand Inquisitor. You would refuse me knowledge of my freedom in exchange for comfort, and thus steal my dignity and potency.*

FEAR: *Can you deny that both humility and wisdom are on the side of the Inquisitor? Yes, I speak with the voice of authority. I echo the commands and prohibitions of your parents. But I speak as your past, your tradition. If I limit you to the possibilities which were conceivable to your parents, it is merely to enforce those rules and limits they found necessary to the fullness of life. My voice is conservative. I would have you love what your fathers loved and hate what they hated, for there is wisdom in the experience of the generations which is absent in the individual. I preserve your energies from being dissipated in folly.*

SK: *The limits of the possible change. Human nature is not static. What was psychologically inconceivable to my parents is an open possibility for me, except when you intervene.*

FEAR: *I am glad you spoke about "the limits of the possible." You are aware that Camus used this phrase as a summary of his philosophy of life. Now—can you tell me in all honesty that you are willing to face the uncertainty, the tentativeness, the absolute demand for self-definition in the face of the absurd that was his daily bread and wine? If not, don't pretend that you want me to leave you altogether, because I protect you against this horrible vacuum of the unknown. I give you ground upon which to stand in the swirl. Even if it is sometimes bitter ground, it is a place for your feet. Better fear than anxiety, better a hostile force at the center of your personality than the emptiness which is the promise of death, better pain than chaos. The suffering I cause is only a necessary by-product of enforcing the limits which give you definition and succor.*

SK: *I do not accept your way. Granted, I must have limits or else I would explode into the void of infinite possibility and schizophrenia. However, there is a better way to establish boundaries than you suggest. Decision is the alternative to fear.*

I can take upon myself the responsibility for deciding, and then the pain of limitation is not imposed but chosen. Maturity rather than fate or fear may determine the shape my life will assume. Your presence is not necessary.

FEAR: *I will admit this heroic possibility exists. Should you choose to accept full responsibility for your values and decisions, I will leave you. But I will always be waiting for your energies to give out. Few persons manage the heroic style of total responsibility. I doubt that you can abide by this high ideal. At any rate, we are talking in theoretical terms. As of this moment, you are still engaged in dialogue with me. If the time comes when you choose to be fascinated by love, or creativity, or even work, I will leave you alone. For the time being we remain reluctant friends.*

SK: *I accept your conclusion with sadness. Nevertheless, I must say, you begin to bore me. Perhaps tomorrow I will converse with you less, and the day after not at all.*

FEAR: *We shall see.*

OCTOBER 10, 1968. DIALOGUE WITH MY SPECTATOR

SK: *Why are you always watching me? Why are your eyes always on me? You observe everything I do. At those times when joy would emerge if only I could act with spontaneity there you are with your clinical gaze, measuring, judging, commenting, making me self-conscious. You rob me of integrity.*

SPECTATOR: *You protest too much.* Specto ergo sum. *It is precisely because I look at you that you know you exist. I keep you from disappearing into unreflective spontaneity. Without my presence you would have no consciousness of time or space. You would be without knowing that you were. Would you really want this kind of animal immediacy? I doubt that you would trade the complications of human self-consciousness for the simplicity you pretend to desire. I may cause you agony but I am also the source of your multiplicity and your glory.*

SK: *Your claims are grandiose and you hide the harm you cause* me in high-sounding words. For instance, what you call multiplicity is a polite word for schizophrenia. I am tired of being two, or three, or four persons. I don't think this homelessness, this duality is the necessary price I must pay for being human. Is it not possible to be one, to be unified, to be whole? Could I not act without self-consciousness?

SPECTATOR: You do me an injustice. Schizophrenia, in the psychological as well as the spiritual sense, cannot be confused with reflective self-consciousness. If you could not get reflective distance from your actions you would be an object and not a person. What you find painful is not my watching you but the look you imagine you detect in my eyes. You see my gaze as harsh and judgmental. Would you object if you thought my eyes were more kindly? If I applauded more often?

SK: I am not sure. Certainly if I felt less like a criminal in the spotlight, or a pupil waiting to be graded, if I felt less small and inferior, my objections would be less strong. But I might resent your presence even if your eyes were accepting. The ideal of spontanity is attractive.

SPECTATOR: Perhaps what you are calling spontaneity is only a form of compulsiveness. If you were rid of me you might find you were a captive of unconscious forces which would be destructive of your long-range good.

SK: I believe the total organism can be trusted to act spontaneously and wisely.

SPECTATOR: You are being hopelessly romantic and naïve. You know enough about the dynamics of the libido and the requirements of society to be aware that pure animal spontaneity destroys the environment that makes the satisfaction of animal needs possible. You need my oversight and wise management. I keep pure vitality from destroying form, the id from destroying the ego, the present from doing violence to the past and the future. I watch over you with kindly intent and try to ensure you the richest and most complete experience over the course of an entire lifetime.

SK: *But your kindly intent so often does violence to my instincts and to the demands of my body. Must we be enemies? Is there no way for you to watch over and guide me without alienating me from myself?*

SPECTATOR: *You might, had you the courage, discover the source of the hatred, judgment, and demanding intent you seem to find reflected in my eyes. Before whose eyes are you small, inadequate, guilty, shameful? If you were to remove these projections from my face, you might discover what rational requirements spring from my oversight. You might find that reflective self-consciousness may be the most concrete mode of self-love. I care for your wholeness. That is why I cannot let you surrender to the moment.*

OCTOBER 21, 1968. DIALOGUE WITH ANGER.

SK: *It has taken me a long time to discover that you are haunting my footsteps. Like a thief dodging from tree to tree, you hide behind other emotions until it is safe to strike. Now I call you by name—Anger, rage, resentment, hatred. Come out into the open and show yourself.*

(No answer)

Anger, I know you are there. Only this morning I was ready to scream at Heather and the children with no just cause. I felt your presence, also, in the way I punished myself with guilt and painful self-consciousness. And I know with what frequency I create an enemy in order to have a target for my free-floating rage. So come out of hiding and state your case.

ANGER: *All right, damn it, I will. Yes, I am here and have been for a long time and it is damn well time you granted me the high honor of diplomatic recognition. Damn generous of you. I was beginning to think you would spend your whole life as a good boy, as a "Christian," as a gentleman, denying my existence. I have been the Red China of your psyche for too long, outlawed, ignored, and cursed. And now you have the gall to pretend to be surprised that I must hide and come* out at what you call "inappropriate" moments. How in hell could I emerge at any other moments?

SK: *Must you be so profane? I have acknowledged that I have denied you rightful recognition. Can't you state your case calmly?*

ANGER: *You are some damn thin-skinned gentleman! You call me out and you are afraid of the slightest suggestion of violence, even verbal violence. What are you afraid of? Who do you think is going to hear me, God or the Devil? Either take me with my profanity and my raw edges or leave me alone and I will find my own ways of emerging.*

SK: *All right, I will try to accept you as you are. Could you begin by telling me something about your origins and your aim?*

ANGER: *I would like to begin with clarity and maturity, but I can't. I have been denied so long I am confused about myself. I don't know where I came from or what would satisfy me. I feel like a hurt child and I want to strike out at you and at other people (particularly those you love) to retaliate for all the years you ignored me.*

SK: *I have already confessed my folly and sorrow in seeking to deny your presence. Let's stop the recriminations and get on with an adult conversation.*

ANGER: *I will try. Let me go back to the beginning. It was not entirely your fault that I was denied a legitimate place in your life. One of the problems with a Christian environment is that it makes aggression and anger shameful. Do you remember, for instance, when you used to fight with your older brother and regularly get beaten up? You were afraid of me. That is why you were defeated. What would have happened if you got angry with your brother? Anger is morally the same as murder, so the New Testament ethic suggests. And do you remember the delicious time when one of your older friends defended you and beat up your brother? Afterward you felt ashamed of being an ally in victory rather than a victim. This seems to be the feeling about life which conservative religion sanctions: better to suffer than rebel. The ideal of love throws anger into question. Turn the other cheek. Be gentle.*

SK: *Well, what is wrong with gentleness? Certainly it is more rewarding than resentment, hatred, fighting, and killing.*

ANGER: *Now wait a minute! There you go jumping to the conclusion that I either drive people to harbor continual resentment or to commit murder. That is a lie you tell yourself in order not to have to deal with me. I can control myself. When not denied my proper recognition I am a very rational emotion. I can distinguish between appropriate and inappropriate objects. Did you ever consider how valuable I am to you?*

SK: *In what ways?*

ANGER: *I keep you safe by making your full strength available to you in situations of danger. I help you to identify those enemies that threaten your well-being. I defend the boundaries of the physical, psychological, economic, and social space you need to survive. And, I might say, I add as much spice to life as your highly idealized love. I keep one person from being swallowed up by another and thus preserve the duality which is necessary for love. If you doubt that I am the companion of love, remember the ecstasy of the reconciliation that comes after fighting. After a good expression of clean anger, lovers have established the integrity of their separateness, and they may come together without fearing that either will be eradicated by the act of love. If you can't fight, you can't love.*

SK: *I agree. I suppose the question I am asking myself is how to maximize the loving and minimize the fighting. I will admit that I would not want to deny you recognition. But you are an exhausting friend to have around. I would like to see you visit less often and on more appropriate occasions.*

ANGER: *Perhaps that is as far as we can go in this conversation. If you will be more sensitive to my comings and goings, I will try to be a more mature and orderly guest.*

· · ·

NOVEMBER 16, 1968. REFLECTIONS ON A BORDER TOWN

Tijuana. Just south of the border. Slightly off limits. South of the industrial revolution. Seedy Dionysus, ecstasy gone to pot. Nothing is neat or fixed. Prices change by the instant. Streets begin and end haphazardly, without reason. Certainly without rhyme. Time is not measured off in discreet units. Tomorrow will be soon enough to tend to yesterday's needs.

No one cares for Tijuana. The machines are dented, the streets pitted, the air polluted. Garbage in the gutters. Beauty is humiliated. And there is vice. And vice versa. The town seems a well-used whore, a trading post for plastic handiwork.

Just off the main street—poverty. Poor is poor, not blessed. Parsimony can be beautiful in a machine or a building. Function performed without frill, lines meeting without excess, make of simplicity an ornament. But life involuntarily reduced to necessity does not rejoice. Poverty makes beauty a luxury. The machine, the finely tuned body of an athlete, the spirit of a seasoned man, are lean, stripped of the superfluous. Fat and malnutrition go together.

NOVEMBER 28, 1968

God, but I want madness!
I want to tremble,
to be shaken,
to yield to pulsation,
to surrender to the rhythm of music and sea,
to the seasons of ebb and flow,
to the tidal surge of love.

I am tired of being
hard,
tight,
controlled,
tensed against the invasion of novelty,

armed against tenderness,
afraid of softness.
I am tired of
directing my world,
making,
doing,
shaping.

Tension is ecstasy in chains.
The muscles are tightened to prevent trembling.
Nerves strain to prevent trust, hope, relaxation.

Surrendering,
giving in to the involuntary is:
madness (idiots tremble),
ecstasy (being out of my skin, what am I?),
bliss (love is coming together and parting),
grace (dancing with the whole spirit).

Surrendering,
giving in to the involuntary is:
insanity (which voices are mine?),
terror (now, who am I?),
torture (aliens are fighting in my brain),
being possessed (by a god or a demon, or both).

Which:
madness or insanity,
trembling or being afraid,
enthusiasm or possession?
The path is narrow to the right madness.
Be wary of trembling in the wrong places!
The demons often disguise themselves as gods.
And vice versa.

· · ·

Surrender is a risk no sane man may take.
Sanity never surrendered is a burden no man may carry.

God, give me madness
that does not destroy
wisdom,
responsibility,
love.

NOVEMBER 29, 1968. FOR ZORBA WITH LOVE

Zorba, forever on my mind. I curse and love you because I am what I am. You hold up a mirror to my sometimes too serious face. Like the boss, I think too much. But there is often dancing in my mind, ideas frolicking. Sometimes my body is moved. Yet I am a careful person, taking thought for the morrow. I don't know how to care without being careful, without remaining faithful to the "full catastrophe" of rootedness in a profession and a family.

But I long to release the gypsy in me who would roam the earth, tasting, sampling, traveling light. There are so many lives I want to live, so many styles I want to inhabit. In me sleeps Zorba's concern to allow no lonely woman to remain comfortless. (Here am I, Lord—send me!) Camus's passion to lessen the suffering of the innocent, Hemingway's drive to live and write with lucidity, and the unheroic desire to see each day end with tranquillity and a shared cup of tea.

I am so many, yet I may only be one. I mourn for all the selves I kill when I decide to be a single person. Decision is a cutting off, castration. I travel one path only by neglecting many. Actual existence is tragic, but fantastic existence (which evades choice and limitation) is pathetic. The human choice may be between tragedy and pathos, Oedipus and Willy Loman. So I turn my back on small villages I will never see, strange flesh I will not touch, ills I will not cure, and I choose to be in the world as a husband, a father, an explorer of ideas and styles of life. Perhaps Zorba will not leave me altogether. I would not like to live without dancing, without unknown roads to explore, without the confidence that my actions were helpful to some.

NOVEMBER 31, 1968. FEAR AGAIN

My ancient fear came last night to pay its monthly visit. It comes less often than it once did and I have come to expect its dreadful face. Still I tremble, tensing my forehead and chest, as if to shutter my house against the danger, in hope that it will pass me by. But fear is drawn to tension like vultures to decay.

Once fear was firmly established in my living room I sat anxiously wondering how long its visit would last. Then I decided to take the initiative, to yield to the fear, to journey deeply into its interior, to find its secret. I imagined a door labeled FEAR in a stone wall. I opened the door and went through into the darkness beyond. The blackness was profound, a moist, throbbing vault. I gave myself to the pulsating darkness and the rhythm gradually became clear. The night was filled with crying. I gasped for breath as each sob shook me. As the world-sorrow inhabited me with each lengthening cycle of sobbing, I came to the bottom of the darkness. The rock on which fear rests, the root of terror is—abandonment. I was alone in the unanswering, unlimited darkness, naked and helpless in the void. My stomach knotted, whirled, and gradually came to rest. The tension began to subside. I went back up through the darkness and out the door in the wall.

Back in my living room, fear was still present, but its face began to change. As I realized that the acid of terror was not strong enough to dissolve my strength, fear passed over into loneliness. I felt I was alone on a raft four thousand miles at sea. But my solitude was pure and strong. It rooted in the essential aloneness I feel when I must bear the burden of my decisions without recourse to any external authority. It seems to me that, loneliness is bearable if it is not identified with abandonment and helplessness. Being alone I may reach out to others, build bridges, risk tenderness, confess need. And if I never learn that perfect love which is said to cast out fear, I may discover enough to allow me to withstand its periodic visits.

NOVEMBER 31, 1968. VOWS

What does it mean to take a vow? Marcel shows how the ethic of spontaneity and momentary sincerity leads to the destruction of identity and how fidelity alone binds our times together. But I think he has not recognized sufficiently the limitation of feeling that may be involved in taking a vow. If I take a vow I bind myself; I place an a priori limit on the way in which my future feelings may be acted upon. I pledge my future to a person or a cause without regard to how I may feel at that time. Is this wisdom or folly?

Without a vow no depth of commitment, trust, or relationship may develop. Yet when a vow is taken I must sometimes force myself to act in a way that does violence to my feelings of the moment. The vow of sexual fidelity in marriage is the clearest example. Loyalty to an institution is a less clear instance. Even within marriage, a vow may become a pretext for mutual possession between spouses. It is not conformity to a vow that creates richness between two, but rather *eros*. I am loved only as I am desired, enjoyed, only as I give spontaneous delight to another. *Agape* may be dehumanizing. Who needs it? However, delight comes and goes. It is mixed with anger, neutrality, boredom, jealousy, compassion, hurt. And how is the judgment to be made whether a relationship contains sufficient delight to justify its continuance? If the relationship is always contingent, on trial, the persons involved are too busy reassuring themselves for delight to develop. Seemingly, delight flourishes best in an atmosphere of trust, commitment, and nonchalance, i.e., within a context which can only be provided by a vow. Is it the case that the deepest tenderness, the most profound ecstasy may develop only when a pledge has been given? Is depth of relationship purchased only at the price of breadth? If so, those feelings which create the richest life require the sacrifice of acting upon many momentary desires. It would seem that we must choose the feelings we will nourish, perhaps even those we will allow.

To take a vow is an awful risk. As is not taking a vow. We must choose where we will allow ourselves to tremble. We must decide which gods we will allow to be born. This is the burden and joy of human freedom.

DECEMBER 1, 1968. DIS-EASE, GRACE, AND PHILOSOPHICAL THOUGHT

It is hard to write today. The dis-ease of the last days is past. I am back in focus. Anxiety and fear are only remembered visitors. I have worked this morning with a stream of ideas at floodtide; writing hurriedly before they pass downstream, shuttling many into hastily built coffer-dams to be used to irrigate in times of dryness. There is a danger in writing a journal that it may be a report only of problems and dis-ease. In my more graceful moments it does not occur to me to report my position to myself or to others. I am simply where I am without any painful self-consciousness which seeks an else-where. Were I completely at ease with myself I might never write. I think now of my early dream of being a rancher. Perhaps in the New Jerusalem, where there will be no church, government, artists, theologians, or philosophers, I may be a graceful rancher. In the meantime, to philosophize is both my dis-ease and my medicine.

There are worse solutions.

DECEMBER 7, 1968. SERENDIPITY

I fell in love with the word "serendipity" long before I knew what it meant. Years ago when I first heard it, I rolled it around on my tongue and smiled at the way it sounded. Somehow I never got around to learning its meaning. Two weeks ago I heard someone use it. I interrupted and asked what it meant. The user did not know. At this point I resolved to search out its meaning. The word and I were fated to come together.

Serendipity: "the gift of finding valuable or agreeable things not sought for." I glanced from the dictionary to the shirt I was wearing which I had found the week before on the highway, and I knew I had found the word that captures my style of life and thought. (Strange, that I should have finished *Apology for Wonder* and not have discovered "serendipity.") I have always been a finder of valuable things which have been lost, abandoned, or despised by others. Some of my favorite clothes have been rescued from the Salvation Army. When I go to New York, I visit the thrift shops before any of the other cultural centers. And, of course, the most numinous place in Boston is not Beacon Hill but Filene's basement. As I walk to work I cross a meadow by the golf course, and lost golf balls which have been hiding in the tall grass creep under my feet so I will find them. (I have found that if I concentrate on looking I find 50 per cent fewer golf balls.) I could go on with a history of my findings—pearls in Shellpot Creek, money on city streets, etc.

I am convinced that a life-style colors all feelings, actions, and aspirations. My style as a philosopher or theologian is also serendipitous. I have always been more interested in the graceful dimensions of the ordinary than in those supposedly crucial events which Christian orthodoxy has focused upon. I find more grace in conversation than in The Word, more in my familial history than in the history of Israel, more in the cool blue of sea and warm of flesh than in worship. When I cease searching and striving, I am always surprised to discover the density and meaningfulness, almost radiance, that ordinary things and actions have. When the quest for salvation is laid aside, a cup of tea with my wife as the sun goes down is as graceful as anything I can imagine. Grace surprises me in modest and hidden places.

DECEMBER 8, 1968. PRAYER

Prayer—a moot, embarrassing, and neglected problem.

To the secular man who assumes that the limits of all human knowledge are known, the issue of prayer is meaningless. Even if there is a God, we cannot know anything about him and it is stupid and impious to address him with petitions and thanksgiving. Prayer can be nothing but an infantile, passive-dependent form of projection of the human need for a personal order onto the empty screen of a careless and impersonal world. It is, at best, a deceptive interior dialogue which may, by way of autosuggestion, create an illusion which has therapeutic value for those who need such ideological crutches.

Even for the person who retains some religious orientation, prayer remains a problem. It seems psychologically essential to address God and yet theologically unnecessary. If God is anything more than mortal, he certainly has no need to be reminded of the needs of his creatures. And it is difficult for most persons to believe that prayer is a one-to-one communication between believer and God (on the model of the telephone conversation).

I can only make several observations.

When I allow myself to pray (which is seldom), I feel very differently from when I am talking to myself. I know the feeling of interior dialogue. In prayer I feel my words going out to the unknown mystery which I trust is the caring context of my existence. I do not find myself in communication with any person. There are no answering words.

I find I must, on occasions, bring my longing, sorrow, joy, anxiety to focus in words and utter them to the unknown source of my existence. And why should I not? I use fantasy, imaginary dramatization, personification in every other area of my life and thought without embarrassment. I write dialogues with fear, ecstasy, with parts of my body, with stones. I inhabit my dream symbols, becoming now an electric stove, a staircase in an old house, or whatever. I address my father who is dead, and I speak to a child named Sammy who is still alive within me. All of the techniques suggested by Gestalt therapy make use of dramatization. And what is prayer but dramatizing my essential human feelings by using the richest metaphors I can discover?

Prayer is a dramatic personalized projection. What else could it be? We who do it are persons and we may speak of the unknown only in language borrowed from the known. No truly religious person thinks there is any strict correlation between his words, images, or symbols and the ultimate reality toward which they are addressed. I remember Tillich saying "God" is a symbol for God.

The real question seems to be: Why should we consider prayer an embarrassing exception to the rule that imagination, fantasy, personification, analogy, and dramatization are invaluable techniques for positioning ourselves creatively in the world?

JANUARY 1, 1969. PROMETHEUS AND JESUS

Something strange and new is moving within me, welling up from the inchoate darkness. I catch a glimpse of it in listening to the *Messiah* when I am inhabited by a structure of completeness, a triumphant and poignant drama which somehow stretches and fills me with a new energy. I sense it also when I find myself able, perhaps for the first time, to read the Gospel of Mark, not as a theological document but as a rich human story. Fifteen years of theological, philosophical and historical analysis of the New Testament left me with no defensible categories by which to understand Jesus. Lacking such handles, I have tended to shy away from the power and mystery of the story. I find a new openness to renew a friendship with a man who once disappointed me deeply by being neither God nor the Savior I trusted him to be during my green years.

Perhaps some of this reaching out to understand the style of existence that is incarnate in Jesus is due to my disillusionment with Prometheus as a model. In an essay on Prometheus in *Raids on the Unspeakable,* Thomas Merton articulates what I have come to understand recently. Prometheus, *the* model of the "modern" consciousness, perpetuates his rebellion, his alienation, and his guilt by assuming that the fire necessary for human life must be stolen from jealous gods. He thus becomes a thief who must live in guilt and anguish for the crime of defying the repressive order imposed by the Olympian gods. To cherish anxiety as the mark of courage, to court doubt as the token of honesty, to remain homeless in the wilderness of the world is to live in the Promethean myth. The price of such loyalty is alienation, becoming an enemy of the self, the world, and the jealous gods. The Christian myth tells another story (although there are echoes of the Promethean myth in Genesis). Man is given fire, freedom, and power by God. God's one desire is that man retain his fire, that he feel the power and the juice of love flowing wildly in his veins, so long as he lives. Thus the Christian must say: "Goddamn all that extinguishes the fire! Goddamn the greed that saps the energies of man to build empires in Vietnam, Czechoslovakia, Tibet, Guatemala. Goddamn all the monuments of stone that rest upon the tortured flesh of living men! Goddamn the sludge (the apathy, the satiety, the impotence) that clogs the red arteries of life." The Christian God is for hot blood, fire, new life, the resurrection of the body. Unfortunately most churches remain gnostic in their attitudes toward the body and the natural world.

Perhaps in this new willingness to see the human potency and sacred mystery of Jesus I am reaching out to reclaim my own fire; I am returning to the life-affirming Christian myth; I am expressing my desire to return from the exile of living in a world which is hostile, alien, and acidic to the human spirit. While I may not forget the reality of tragedy and death, I would nevertheless like to wander in this wilderness of a world, trusting that the mystery which is my source and goal conspires with me to keep the fire alive.

JANUARY 1, 1969. MAN—CORRUPT OR IMMATURE?

There is an immense theoretical as well as functional difference between the view that man is corrupt and therefore in need of salvation and the view that he is immature or weak and needs to grow up. If the human predicament is seen as serious, critical, a matter of life and death, then radical therapy is not only appropriate but morally necessary. If, on the other hand, the difference between the best and the worst of men is a matter of degrees rather than of kind, the therapy prescribed for the ailing will be less severe. Traditional Christianity, romanticism, Marxism, and the hippies see a radical discontinuity between sinner and saved, corrupt and innocent, exploiter and exploited, the square and the hip. Each calls for some form of radical therapy: conversion, new birth, ideological revolution, turning on, becoming enlightened, passing from darkness into light. Depth psychology, humanistic wisdom, and common sense see the indefinite shades of gray that distinguish the wise and the foolish, the mature and the immature. They know the darkness that remains in the hearts of the enlightened as well as the moments of lucidity and kindness that surprise the dullest of human beings. Growth rather than conversion is therefore the remedy they prescribe for all men.

JANUARY 15, 1969. THE AMATEUR STATUS OF PHILOSOPHY AND THEOLOGY

A theologian who cannot remain an amateur should get out of the profession! Professionalism has killed the profession— learned men (without biographies) talking with one another in bloodless dialogues; repeating the opinions of authorities sancti-

fied by tradition or ecclesiastical popularity; never taking the
risk of speaking from the precarious position of their private
experience of life.

My anger has been simmering for three days. The editors of
a *serious* theological journal published by a seminary one block
and one hundred years removed from an ivy university have
consistently refused to publish any of my essays. They returned
"Reflections on a Peach-Seed Monkey" this week with the
following critique given by one of their anonymous editorial
readers:

On the whole, it seems to me Sam writes rather well, and
his problem is not with his style, but at two other points:
first, his tendency to be rather cute, or to come at things from
the side, and, second, his failure to speak consistently to any
particular reading public. I don't think I need to document the
point about being cute or coming at things from the side. One
can see this from his article, even in its title. It is a kind of
advertising device of the kind which, if in good taste, might have
some point in a sermon, but it seems to me more likely to irritate
serious theological readers.

The other point is related to it, but is more subtle. On the one
hand, Sam cites all the radical theologians and various other
people in a way that expects his readers to be fully familiar with
them all, but when he comes to his own message, he speaks to the
reader as if the reader was almost devoid of critical ability. In
other words, it seems to me that the failure to identify the reader
who is his target for the piece, gives him two quite different levels
of discussion, so that he will irritate the one, and confuse the other.

If Sam wants this material to be read by a wider public, then
I think he will have to curb his penchant for name-dropping.

It is true that I don't actually think much about his conclusion,
but comments are made quite apart from the validity of his thesis.

Finally, the basic level of thought that underlies the paper, it
seems to me, is unimpressive. It is a little premature, in my

judgment, to concede the whole field to the radical theologians.

The anger of continual rejection aside, there is a serious theological issue at stake. What is theology? Or to put the question in a more functional way: What does that phrase "thinking theologically" (which is the darling of the new curriculum planners at seminaries) mean? This question is being left unanswered. Until recently, thinking theologically has meant (1) thinking biblically, (2) thinking traditionally, and (3) thinking ecclesiastically. Both Barth and Tillich concur with the tradition of ecclesiastical theology which insists that theological thinking is done from within the circle of those who confess the Lordship of Jesus Christ and stand under the authority of the Bible and the tradition of the church. Theology of this genre has always begun with a large number of "truths" which were attested by revelation—broadly or narrowly understood. Thus there has been a standard way of approaching existential and moral problems. Standing firmly on certified truths, the theologian had only to extrapolate the implications of revelation for the contemporary situation. So long as the category of revelation is maintained, theology can be approached from the front, head on, and it need not get involved with the messy data of individual experience.

It is *my* conviction (I will not cite the authority of "the modern mind" or the "empirical temper of the technological man") that this classical, ecclesiastical, revelational notion of theology is inadequate if not downright dangerous because *it begs the question of authority and responsibility.* To the degree that I accept the principles of my faith from the opinions, conclusions, dicta of any external authority, I am living out another person's life. To begin with a model for life which is introjected on the recommendation of an authority is to sell my soul for a role. I assume a "personality" but I lose the ability to grow as a person by continually evaluating my expanding experience. This remains true whether the model

I introject is sanctioned by the authority of my father, Richard Nixon, John Calvin, St. Paul, or even my beloved Zorba.

Thus, it seems to me (a vulnerable phrase,) authentic theology must "come at things from the side." It is necessarily a testimony of biographical experience reflected upon and offered for public reflection. Its conclusions will often be partial, premature, and unimpressive to those who judge by the standards of the traditional system. To those accustomed to the splendor of The Castle, a bungalow built out of native materials will always seem too modest to be interesting. But to the man who constructs his home with his own hands, with no authorized blueprint, no precut lumber, a bungalow is a triumph. To discover a principle (such as the idea of promises in "Peach-Seed Monkey") which gives unity and power to personal action, is to find one of those holy places where one trembles with the assurance of the sanctity of life. Such a discovery is an accomplishment, or a grace, which is not to be despised. I trust that any reader who is in touch with the agonizing character of the search for principles will have some appreciation of the peach-seed monkey. The reader I had in mind could be a professional theologian so long as he was an amateur human being; living, charting his unique pathway through the wilderness with a few companions but without official maps provided by the ecclesiastical A.A.A.

FEBRUARY 1, 1969. THE FUNCTIONAL SIGNIFICANCE OF BELIEF IN GOD

To say "God is" with the total self (or at least a majority of the voices which make up the assembly we call a person) is functionally equivalent to affirming the following with the mind and the guts:

1. I am O.K. as I presently am, not as I was or as I might be.
2. I do not have to make or remake myself.
3. Imperfection is the condition of *authentic* human life.

4. Striving for perfection, for immortality (the perfect is changeless, therefore deathless), for conformity to an image of what I *should* be is idolatry, the effort to turn the temporal into the eternal.

5. The ultimate significance, meaning, security, value, dignity of my life is not dependent upon anything I can do, make, or accomplish. Therefore, my action may spring out of what I am rather than arising out of a desperate need to establish myself. I am already founded, rooted, grounded in (depth metaphors) or contexted and encompassed by (metaphors of inclusion) that which guarantees my integrity.

5. I am not in need of salvation, of radical alteration. Therefore I am set free to change.

7. Authentic life is not governed by the spirit of seriousness. It is graceful, light, and playful.

Zorba is right. It takes more than a touch of madness to affirm such things in the chronological-technological twentieth century of constipated, achievement-oriented makers and doers. We have accomplished so much, humanized so much of the earth, made life easier and more secure. But then there is Los Angeles—the logical end (*telos* and *anus*) of the efforts of *Homo faber*—orderly subdivisions joined by rationally engineered freeways encompassed by pollution.

I wonder, is it a natural law of life that when we strive anxiously to impose the rule of willfulness over our environment (internal or external) to control everything, that we inevitably generate poisons which destroy life?

FEBRUARY 3, 1969. I-WE, THE PRIVATE AND THE PUBLIC, SOLI-
TARINESS AND TRANSCENDENCE, RELIGION
AND POLITICS

I am beginning to understand the primal connection between the religious impulse and political consciousness. Whitehead

said: "Religion is what a man does with his solitariness."
The more I come into touch with my essential aloneness, the
more aware I become of the necessity for community. The
polarity I-We is no less primal than the I-Thou or the I-It,
of which Buber spoke. If I do not transcend myself and discover my identity as one who is encompassed in a We, I become
increasingly prey to illusion, despair, and impotence.

Let me begin with the issue of illusion. Experiments have
shown that a subject (not person) isolated from sensory
stimulus and social interchange begins to hallucinate rapidly
and to lose all sense of reality. Sadists who subject prisoners
to solitary confinement understand intuitively that the cruelest
punishment is to remove a man from the community and thereby deprive him of his humanity. Deprived of a We, the I has no
standard by which to judge his perceptions, to discriminate
between what is inside and what is outside, subjective and objective, illusion and reality. Confusion results when community
is lost.

Potency likewise depends upon community. Bruno Bettel-
heim's studies of autistic children (*The Empty Fortress*) show
what happens when a child is forced to live in an environment
which is totally unresponsive to his efforts to affect and change
it. Health depends upon the conviction that our actions count.
I remain potent only so long as I get feedback which demon-
strates that the force of my action is felt. When I cast my stone
into the water, I must be able to see the waves radiate out-
ward. If I remain in my solitariness, I am denied the knowledge of the resonance of my actions, as well as the joy of
knowing that my gifts are received and appreciated. If my
being and my doing are to be reconciled, if I am to be responsible in my action, I must discover that part of my identity
which only a corporation, a We, a community can guarantee.
I must discover the point at which the blood of my body
(*corpus*) intermingles with a corporation. Potency depends
upon knowing to what body I belong. Intercourse is incorpora-

tion. Love is joining two bodies; it is therefore political. In solitude there is neither love nor politics.

Hope, also, is dependent upon the We. If I choose to remain alone I minimize the flow of outgoing and incoming energy. I hoard my resources and calculate every expenditure. I sow no seeds which I will not harvest. I prepare for no future I will not share. I invest in no corporation which does not pay immediate dividends. Hope cannot live on such a hand-to-mouth basis. It demands a more generous and less calculating attitude. Only if I belong to a We which will eventually reap the fruits of my labors will I trouble myself to plant what I will not reap.

My solitariness must be invested in a people. The energy of my body must flow into a corporation. My love must be decentralized; it must become political.

MAY 28, 1969. FREEDOM

One of the most intoxicating features of this jubilee year has been my discovery of a new dimension of freedom and, therefore, potency. I have learned, to a large degree, to replace "I can't" with "I won't," "I don't want to," "It is not worth the energy and trouble," "There are things I would rather do," or "I don't choose to." In other words, I have had a switch from *seeing* myself as a quasi-determined *victim* to *feeling* myself as a responsible *agent*. With this change has come a sense that the future is open. Within certain limits which are *given* (gifts), I may do and become what I want. The ethical question has changed for me from "What ought I to do?" to "What is most deeply satisfying to my total self?" (To shortcut the inevitable criticisms of subjectivism, let me say that I understand myself to be essentially in a social context and therefore my fundamental desires always involve other persons).

This new sense of freedom has changed the way I think about emotion, feeling, and desire. Like most people, I had assumed I was a victim of emotions. Moods came and went like the wind, and the only course of wisdom was to relax and go with the feeling of the moment. I now think such a view was a subtle romantic ideology which relieved me of the responsibility for my style of life. It allowed me the luxury of being a victim of forces over which I supposedly had no control.

Of course, there is no theoretical way of proving that I am free to choose the way I feel. But clearly, if I believe I am not responsible for my feelings, I will be unable to do anything to change them. And, contrariwise, if I assume I am responsible (since my feelings are a reflection of a total style of life I have chosen) I cease to be a victim. Since the issue cannot be solved theoretically, it seems sensible to adopt the view of the emotions which promises the greatest freedom. I have no choice but to act *as if* I were responsible for my feelings if acting in this way allows me to change my feelings in a desired manner.

Let me be specific. For years I struggled with a manic-depressive style of life. When I was elated I would work, love, and play with abandon and before long would exhaust my energies. Then I would suffer a season of dryness and disaffection. I assumed that this cycle of feelings was a part of the given structure of my personality type which could only be accepted. Wisdom required that I resign myself to fated patterns. I now believe this is wrong. A closer analysis of the manic-depressive cycle shows it is based upon the assumption that all good feelings must be paid for by an equal amount of bad feelings. This assumption, in turn, rests upon the judgment that I ought not be too happy. There is something virtuous, desirable, or secure about suffering.

It is easy enough to see how such assumptions and judgments arise. They are deeply imbedded in the Protestant ethic and are reinforced by the extra-solicitous care we all receive as children when we are sick or feel bad. Feeling bad is an almost automatic way for a child to gain the caring attention of parents. Unfortunately many of us carry this self-defeating pattern into

adult life and dignify the suffering we cause ourselves with religious, philosophical, or psychological theories about the nature
of man which assure us that man is *essentially* estranged from
himself. It is human nature for man to be divided against himself.

I have a growing conviction that the Christian presence in
Western civilization has perpetuated a disease in order to offer
a cure. It has encouraged schizophrenia by insisting that man
is a sinner (estranged from self, others, nature, and God)
who can do nothing to save himself. Indeed, all attempts at
self-help are indications of pride which only deepen sin. The
word "Pelagian" has been used to anathematize those who
believe human freedom is potent. From Paul to Augustine to
Luther to Barth to Bultmann, we have been told man in his
actual historical condition is fallen and is not free. It is only
by the intervention of grace, which is (in some mysterious way)
mediated by Jesus Christ, that freedom is restored and estrangement overcome. Nor is it possible, as liberals attempt in every
generation, to remove the idea of vicarious atonement from
the heart of the gospel. The hard core of Christian tradition
has always insisted upon the impotence and bondage of the
human will. It has said loud and clear—"You can't. You can't
heal yourself. Your only hope is in accepting *the* physician
sent from God" (whose credentials are certified by the church).

There is increasing (soft) evidence which suggests that
reliance upon an exterior medium of salvation (whether the
nostrum offered be church, state, psychiatrist, astrologist,
Timothy Leary, Black Panthers, or some guru recently arrived
from the East) fosters a passive-dependent style of life in
which the responsibility for personal growth is evaded. This we
know about psychopathology—at the heart of "illness" is the
impotent child who is still crying, "I can't. You do it for me."
And, it is clear that the moment in therapy when the patient
begins to "get well' is when he says, "I am responsible for my
feelings, my actions and my style of life. In spite of parents,

family, friends or the surrounding culture, I alone can make
the decision to outgrow my dis-ease and to establish a way of
life that is satisfying. There is no magic. There is no automatic
dispenser of grace. There are no saviors. My final dignity is in
my ability to choose my style of life."

I find it painful but necessary to make a radical choice at this
point between the church and the gospel. At the center of the
tradition of the church has been the doctrine of vicarious atonement and the encouragement of a passive-dependent life-style.
I reject this magical view of salvation. But there is a gospel
the church has seldom seen and perhaps is systematically pre-
vented from seeing by the necessity to maintain an organization.
Dostoevski captures its essence in the legend of the Grand
Inquisitor. The Good News is: "You are free and you will find
yourself becoming graceful as you assume the responsibility for
yourself and others." It is increasingly my experience that the
dignity of human life resides in its potential for radical freedom. Each human being is free to choose how he will feel
about and be in the world. No saviors are necessary to confer
this freedom. We need, rather, witnesses who will be lucid in
their acceptance of the universal human birthright of the gift
of radical freedom.

JUNE 2, 1969. GRACEFUL AWAKENING
Yesterday morning I awoke and started to get out of bed but,
remembering it was Sunday, decided to settle back and simmer
a while. For some time I listened to the ocean waves (distant
and fuzzy sounding—low tide—not good for surfing). Gradually I became aware of the sea breeze flowing over my body.
Unhurriedly I savored dapple-gray sky, sheets on skin, Lael
humming, the smell of cooking bacon. Musingly my mind ran
forward in time and began to play with the possibilities of
the day. I called the alternatives before me and sampled each
until I was able to determine what activities promised the most

satisfaction. Having settled on a tentative plan for the day, I allowed the moving air to caress me once more, dressed, and followed the smell of cooking bacon to its source.

Afterward, in remembering my manner of awakening, I was struck with a sense of thanksgiving so strong that I felt like singing a hymn. My joy was created not only by this morning, but by the realization that for several months I had been awakening with awareness and anticipation rather than with anxiety. For most of my life it had been my custom to begin the day by carefully assuming the burden of my ancient fears and inadequacies, and by planning the tasks which must be performed. I clothed myself with estrangement each morning as automatically as I dressed my body. Until recently, I have not been willing to drop this dreadful burden. Freedom was too threatening.

> *(BYRON: My very chains and I grew friends,*
> *So much a long communion tends*
> *To make us what we are.)*

And now it is happening. I allow myself to be happy.

I think this experience of graceful awakening says more clearly than the entry of May 28 what I understand to be the relationship between grace and freedom. Grace is being willing to be your whole self. It is true that no one of us can coerce himself out of the condition of estrangement by "will power." But the issue of whether or not we are responsible for our estrangement is not the issue of will power. What we normally understand by will power is the compulsive strength of one part of the personality trying to impose its desires on the whole. I can try to repress my fears by will power, but it does no good because the repressed part of the personality grows more powerful by being denied. If, on the other hand, I end the tyranny of one aspect of my personality over the other (whether the tyrant is libido, ego, or superego, child, parent or adult, underdog, topdog, etc.) I allow multiplicity to exist within myself. Grace results from being willing to risk living without repression of embarrassing images, feelings, desires. When repression lessens, we are always surprised to learn that we have been more afraid of the angel of happiness than the demons we have kept chained in the dark prison of the psyche.

Graceful freedom is having the courage to be satisfied.

JUNE 27, 1969. SILENCE: AGNOSTICISM AND TRUST
I have been aware recently of the growing presence of silence within me. There are moments when the interior dialogue ceases, when judging, analyzing, comparing, synthesizing, etc., slow to a halt and quietness infiltrates my consciousness. At such times nothing calls for an explanation, no words are necessary to complete an otherwise incomplete situation. Things are what they are and I am too involved in wondering *at* them to question *why* they are as they are. I am even less inclined to talk *about* them.

I had a semicomic vision the other day that captures something of the significance of silence. In comparing my sometimes anxious anticipation of future events to a silent waiting upon the future to emerge, I remembered an old Walt Disney cartoon. Sylvester the cat is running away from his ancient enemy the bulldog. Suddenly he sees that the only way of escape open to him is across a pond. Without hesitating he runs out onto the water with no worry about sinking. So long as he remains unanxious, a lily pad arises to meet each of his advancing feet a split second before he would otherwise sink into the water. Suddenly, he becomes alarmed, for although his feet have found support for his journey thus far he can see no visible means of support for the remainder of the trip across the pond. The moment he begins to worry whether the next lily pad will appear on schedule, he sinks into the water and the bulldog stands on the shore and laughs. Quiet anxiety and the world appears as a continuous series of happenings. When I cease asking for guarantees that my feet will find secure ground, support appears for my advancing steps. The trick is to stop demanding certainty and trust in the ability of the self to respond creatively to whatever happens. You can't be graceful looking at your feet! Trust the happenings.

There is another facet of this experience of silence. I find myself increasingly unwilling to speak about what is sacred to me. The more I am struck with the poignancy and wonder of being alive, the less I want to talk about God or about theology. The reality in which this gift of my life is rooted is too mysterious and too sacred to be spoken about in familiar terms. It seems a sacrilege to talk about God, to patter on as if we knew what we were talking about, to gab and gossip about attributes and acts of God as if we had some secret knowledge of the ultimate mystery.

I think I would like to define the philosophical position I prefer at the moment as *trustful agnosticism.* I accept my life in wonder as a gift to be enjoyed responsibly, but I remain ignorant about the totality which is my ultimate context. I aspire to trust myself to the happenings which interweave with my energies to form an incarnate and situated person. I am not uncomfortable in saying that my trust in the ultimate context of my life is invested in God, provided the word "God" is not used more than once a year and is then handled like the Ark of the Covenant.

It would be interesting to see what would happen if theologians would recover the essential reverence of the tradition of negative theology and would understand their role not as "service to the word" (a Barthian concept) but as guardians of silence. In the modern world, we desperately need to discover appropriate ways to say "Take off your shoes—you are on holy ground; allow silence, you are in the presence of a sacred mystery!"

It all depends upon
trusting
silence

and

laughing
because
It must be said.

Five

The Importance of Being Carnal— Notes for a Visceral Theology

I | Carnality and Grace

In the darkness there were demons: fears and injuries from my ancient past taking faces in dreams and returning to haunt my flesh and destroy my hope. Tossing and turning in exile, my spirit wandered in the midnight kingdom of despair and emptiness. But it is morning now. The spirit gradually returns to the flesh. Sitting with my face toward the sea, the gentle heat of the young sun spreads across my back and massages my shoulders. The rhythmic pounding of the waves, wild and loud, cradles and rocks my spirit and returns it to sanity. (I owe a libation to Poseidon.) As my eyes strain to penetrate the horizon, the endless blue and abidingness of the sea triggers my awareness of the eternal space which is the context of my life. I yield myself to the mystery that is my abiding place with cool trust. My breathing becomes measured and slow, my body relaxes. The demons are gone. The day begins gracefully.

What has happened to me? How am I to understand this warmth and grace which pervade my body? As I begin to reflect I realize that neither the Christian nor the secular cultures, in which I have been jointly nurtured, have given me adequate categories to interpret such an experience. Neither has taught me to discern the sacred in the voice of the body and the language of the senses. In the same measure that Christian theology has failed to help me appreciate the *carnality* of grace, secular ideology has failed to provide me categories for understanding the *grace* of carnality. Before I can understand what I have experienced, I must see where Christian theology and secular ideology have failed me.

In spite of the denials of sophisticated theologians to the contrary, Christianity has never escaped from that ancient and perennial dualism (equally manifest in Platonism, gnosticism, and schizophrenia) which considers the flesh of less dignity than the spirit and the senses inferior to the mind. In recent years we have heard a great deal about the Hebrew idea of the psychosomatic unity of man. Gradually a modicum of celebration of the senses has infiltrated the church. It is now permissible to enjoy a properly legalized sex life with a clear Christian conscience, and art and dance are beginning to find their way back into the sanctuary. But in spite of these minor steps forward there remains a deep-seated suspicion of the carnal enthroned in the Christian understanding of history and salvation. Nothing less than a major theological revolution will allow Christianity to escape from the heresy of gnosticism.

According to the theological consensus that has governed Western Christendom, true grace, healing, or salvation is dependent upon recognizing and confessing the Lordship of Jesus Christ and accepting the authoritative witness of the church that he is the revelation of the nature and purpose of God. Thus salvation in the fullest sense involves a form of historical knowledge which is possible only to the person who is in-corporated into the community of Israel. Memory rather than awareness is the crucial faculty for arriving at graceful truth.

The notable thing about this traditional Christian version of what heals and saves is that it places the nostrum for human ills at a distance twice removed from the contemporary existing individual. In order to arrive at the definitive saving act of God which is the source of grace, the existing individual must turn aside from (1) his immediate bodily sensations, (2) his involvement in nature, (3) his current cultural and political situation, and take a trip back into the history of ancient Israel. Characteristically, Protestantism has declared that healing comes not from what may be seen, or felt, or touched but from *hearing* the word of God. The ear is the organ of salvation. To the person whose ears are closed to hearing of God's mighty acts in the history of Israel, there can be no adequate understanding of grace. Attention to the body (sensations and feelings), to the beauty and grandeur of nature, or to the miracle of human love is not sufficient to understand the grace of God if one has not been initiated into the history of Israel.

When Christian theology locates the *sine qua non* for the authentic life at so great a distance from the incarnate and situated existence of any contemporary man, it subtly devalues the immediate in favor of the mediate, the now in favor of the then, feeling and sensation in favor of obedience to the authority which preserves the crucial memory. Thus no shallow pronouncements about the "psychosomatic unity of man" or "glorifying God with our bodies" or "the celebration of the senses" is able to eradicate the deep rejection of bodily and situated existence that is at the heart of the traditional Christian notions of history and salvation. Unless we are able to locate the presence of that which heals and saves *in contemporary history,* on the soil of what is immediately experienceable, unless we are able to get away from the idea that obedience (intellectual or moral) to some external authority that testifies to having heard THE WORD is the prerequisite for healing, we will not be able to understand that grace which comes from the viscera and which is available wherever beauty or tenderness may be found—in a flower in a crannied wall, or in the morning sun on a California beach. Incarnation, if it is anything more than a "once-upon-a-time" story, means grace is carnal, healing comes through the flesh. The primary locus of the "action of God" is in the viscera, not in ancient Israel! Otherwise, how may I understand that grace which sometimes overtakes me in looking at the sea, or in making love?

At this point an image intrudes itself into my imagination. I see smirking, half-triumphant smiles on the faces of several of my most secularized friends. And now the smiles give way to words:

Of course the antiquated notions of Christianity cannot help you understand your own bodily existence. Only a naturalistic and completely secular view of man can enable you to take full possession of your own feelings and body. You can be *in touch* with the world only if you give up all mystical notions of the body and become the "naked ape" the evolutionary process has made you. You must give up all dualistic notions and realize that you are nothing but your bod. And your body is nothing more than an intricate but closed nexus of interacting chemical and electrical systems which operate in terms of stimulus and response, cause and effect. What you call your mind or spirit is really only your brain, and your "free will" is an illusion that no mechanistic view of the body can support. If you will stop striving toward some fancied transcendence and confess your identity with your body you will be a good and happy animal. You will be in no need of grace because you will not be alienated from your body or your environment.

While such a secular view does far greater justice to the

carnal and situated character of human existence than does the traditional Christian view, it neglects the element of grace in common experience.

By grace I mean something concrete which may be described either poetically or phenomenologically. If it is too inexact to speak of the succoring and healing offered by the sun and the sea, let me define grace as "a sudden reorganization, in a more economical manner, of perceptions, attitudes, and dispositions which results in a relaxation of inner and outer conflicts and in liberation of previously bound energies for projects and relationships which are satisfying to the maturing self." In the contemporary idiom, grace is a happening rather than an achievement, a gift rather than a reward. By lessening the alienation between self and self, self and others, self and world, it creates the possibility of action which is integral and responsible; it sets the self free from compulsive reaction to the past for a present and a future containing genuine novelty. One other aspect of grace must be noted. It happens to an individual who bears a unique biography and destiny and not to an anonymous body governed by the imperative of autonomous laws. I may speak of grace only in the first person.

How adequate the concepts of law, stimulus and response, cause and effect may finally prove for dealing with the totality of human experience is difficult to say at this point in history. However, it is clear that within the integrity of subjective experience there are moments when we find ourselves gratuitously liberated from hurts, habits, and hang-ups which shaped our past and recent present. In such moments it is *as if* law had given way to novelty. When grace happens it is *as if* the sun and the waves had marshaled their resources to dispel those demons which are unique to my biography. While the semi-fantastic category of the *as if* may be inadequate to a scientific description of human conduct, it is indispensable for describing the interior or subjective dynamics of experience. Phenomenology rests upon the *as if,* upon suspending judgment and describing experience as it is lived.

Of course it is always possible, after the fact, for some objective observer to say to the person reporting an experience of the grace of the carnal:

What you experienced as grace, as freedom resulting from the opening of novel possibilities was really only a new Gestalt created by the operation of stimuli and laws which are, in principle, fully understandable. Had we exact enough information about your chemical, physical, and environmental past, we could have predicted the event you insist upon describing in the dubious philosophical categories of grace and freedom. It may seem, for instance, that the so-called "graceful conduct" of the concentration-camp saint who spends his last strength and gives his meager rations to feed those who are worse off than himself is violating all we know about the laws of self-preservation. However, this is not the case. It is merely that his ego needs, which are no less law-governed than biological needs, are strong enough that he is forced to set aside his immediate physical needs.

It is interesting how such deterministic theories of man are able to repair all their failures at prediction by post-diction. If faith in the omnipotence of law does not yield accurate prediction, one may always *ex post facto* abstract certain regularities and continuities from the unexpected event and formulate a new law governing the situation. While such Monday-morning quarterbacking yields little in accurate predictions of when novel Gestalts will take place in an individual's future life, it as least preserves the determinists' faith in law.

In whatever manner we may finally come to relate the interior and the exterior, the existential and the scientific perspectives on experience, one thing is certain—neither can be ignored without doing violence to the way human beings inhabit their world. The subjective or existential experience of carnal grace is a datum which must be accounted for in any adequate view of man. Thus the ideology of secularism is as much in need of correction as is Christian theology if we are to understand bodily existence and the grace we sometimes experience when we come to our senses.

The whole question of the body must be reconsidered with a concerted effort to leave aside the presuppositions of both Christian and secular ideologies and to pay close attention to the sensuous feel of bodily existence. I propose in the remainder of this chapter to (1) look at the implications of incarnate existence, (2) examine the experiential links between the carnal and the sacred, and (3) draw some pragmatic conclusions for theology and religious institutions.

II | *The Implications of Incarnation*

There is a perennial temptation to deny that flesh enters into the essential definition of man. As far back as we have records of man's effort to understand himself, we can trace a strand of dualistic thinking which separates body from soul, flesh from spirit, historical existence from an eternal faculty of reason. Inevitably in such dualism the essence of man is identified with soul, spirit, or reason; and bodily situated existence is seen as an accidental predicate somehow added to the definition of man. With minor variations the major religions of the world have shared this perspective with idealistic philosophy.

It is to the credit of existential philosophy that it has rejected all such efforts to remove the flesh from the definition of man. With increasing clarity from the time of Kierkegaard to the present, man has been defined as a being who is *essentially incarnate and situated.* Body, place, and historical limitations are not mere qualifiers of a timeless human reason. As Marcel has noted, a man *is* his body and his situation. Thus we must be careful of being seduced by the dualism implicit in our language which permits us to speak of "having a body" (as if the possessor and the possessed were different entities). All human knowledge, value, and aspiration is stamped with the mark of the body. The existentialist insight into the incarnate nature of human existence may be stated in these propositions: *A man's body is his bridge to and model of the world; therefore, as a man is in his body so will he be in the world.*

Perhaps the best model to use in thinking about the intimate relationship between body and world is the analogy of the relationship between child and mother. In the beginning is unity, the oneness of the body and the matrix which nurtures and supports it; the embryo and the placenta are inseparable. It is only in a physical sense that birth and the severing of the umbilical cord separate the baby from the mother. According to most hypotheses about infant consciousness, the neonate lives in a state of undifferentiated consciousness. He does not categorize or experience his own lips, the breast of the mother, and the swaddling clothes as belonging to three different spheres of reality (self-other-world, or I-Thou-It). The distinction between self and world comes only as the baby begins to play with his own body and to discover that there are some objects (e.g., feet) which hurt when they are hit and others (e.g., blocks) which do not. Gradually the child discovers that he has control over some things but not over others. If a foot is hurting he can move it and get relief but if a block is requested to move closer to the crib so it can be picked up it remains strangely unresponsive. Out of this dialectic between potent action and frustrated demand, the body is distinguished from the world. However, the distinction is not nearly so absolute as it later becomes. For the child, the objects in the world are still *like* himself; they have feelings, intentions, and even personalities. Thus chairs that trip toddlers are held responsible and punished for their malevolent intent, just as Teddy-bears that comfort are rewarded for their purity of heart.

We might define the end of childhood as that point when the porous membrane which separates the body and the world begins to calcify and alienation between self-body and world sets in. The child learns that he has a body which must be disciplined and controlled if he is to receive adult approval and that the world is primarily to be used rather than enjoyed.

The degree of alienation will depend upon how much the child's family and culture demand that he suppress the desires of his body in favor of the realization of other goals. As Freud pointed out, civilization inevitably involves discontent and alienation. The adult's relation to his body will parallel his relation to the world; whether he trusts or mistrusts, enjoys or seeks to utilize, feels potent or weak, will be equally reflected in his attitude toward his own body and the objective world.

There are powerful forces working against any full acceptance of incarnate existence. The alienation between a man and his body which has been a dominant feature of all societies is not perpetuated without having great survival value. To ignore the body is to cultivate the illusion of immortality. Souls, spirits, and discarnate intelligences are not limited by the conditions of time or space; they easily transcend the threat of pain and nothingness which haunts the flesh. The body is fully experienced only at the price of the loss of any omnipotent perspective and the acceptance of limitation, historicity, and death as belonging essentially to the human condition. While such an acceptance is easy to make on a theoretical level, it is far more difficult to homogenize into the attitudes which shape one's commerce with the world.

The factor governing full incarnation is the willingness to trust that which cannot be controlled. The moment I identify myself with my body and become fully incarnate I involve the

essence of what is me with something over which I have no
ultimate control. If I listen to the voice of the body it is clear
that feeling and sensation have a logic of their own that is
not always responsive to the will. Likewise, the body has its
seasons of ebb and flow, impotence and potency, sickness and
health, and finally life and death. Only as I am able to accept
this rhythm am I able to become fully identified with my body.
As I trust or mistrust the rhythm of my body, so I trust or
mistrust my total world. It is not true that I am cut off from
the rhythms of the natural world. Many sociologists as well
as philosophers want to argue that when Western man ceased
to live in daily communion with the soil, when he ceased to
grow corn and wait for the rains, he necessarily lost his involvement in nature. This is nonsense. The vitality of the sense of
participation in nature is not dependent upon an agricultural
economy. The body is my point of entry into nature, as it is
my bridge to the human world. Trust in the seasons of the
cosmos arises from trust in the rhythms of the body. Gnosticism,
in any of its forms, always views both the body and the cosmos
as alien to man, just as romanticism, on the other hand, views
both nature and the body as trustworthy.

If we lose the self we lose the other; if we lose the body we
lose the world. Thus the danger of not loving one's body. Love
of both neighbor and cosmos rests upon love of self. But even
more, the sacred rests upon the carnal. To an analysis of that
relation we now turn.

III | *The Carnal and the Sacred*

Religious persons frequently fear that acceptance of a fully
incarnate and situational view of man would destroy the idea
of the sacred. If man is totally identified with his body and his
situation, what of the spirit, what of transcendence, what of

commerce with that sacred dimension of reality which has always been symbolized in theology? If we limit man to the time and space of his carnal existence, do we not thereby deny the possibility of his knowing anything of the sacred or speaking of a God who transcends the world?

We may begin to answer these questions by giving the term "sacred" some meaning that is not hopelessly vague. According to Rudolf Otto's classical phenomenological description, the holy is *mysterium: tremendum et fascinans,* a mystery which is at once tremendous-awesome-frightening and fascinating-compelling-desirable. As the source of all value, the holy is in principal inviolable. One therefore trembles in its presence because it presents an absolute demand for recognition and reverence. The holy is also desirable and fascinating because it is the source of all that heals and succors man.

Traditionally man has confronted the holy through the mediation of religious symbols and institutions. In raising the question of the relation between the carnal and the sacred we are suggesting that there may be "nonreligious" experiences of the sacred. The sacred is homogenized into ordinary experience. We have already shown that there is an element of succor and healing in certain sensuous experiences. There is grace in the harmony of color and in caressing winds as well as in words of friendship and the conversation of flesh and flesh. Succor is available from the senses for the man who has not been made blind by resentment. There is, likewise, something in common experience which corresponds to the element of absolute demand, of unconditional oughtness, in the traditional experience of the holy. Let me illustrate.

A picture from a recent newspaper showed a Vietnamese captive being tied behind a jeep. The caption explained that he was going to be dragged through the brush and stubble until he broke and gave his captors the information they wanted. As the impact of the picture began to seep into my body a conversation developed between my viscera and my mind.

VISCERA: *Uu. Pu. I'm sick. I want to throw up. Outrage! Sacrilege! Goddamn it! How can something that walks like a man do this to our flesh?*

MIND: *Hey, What is all this ruckus and profanity about? Why are you threatening rebellion and vomiting and all that?*

VISCERA: *Goddamn it man, do something! We are being tortured. Our flesh is being violated. How can you sit there so calmly when a sacrilege is being committed?*

MIND: *Now wait a minute. Calm down and let's talk this over. Get a little bit of distance from this "event." You are all mixed up. Look at the way you are using pronouns. You say, "We are being tortured." You are right here in good American comfort and security. Furthermore, the guy being tortured is a* North *Vietnamese, or at least a Viet Cong sympathizer. You shouldn't get so riled up.*

VISCERA: *What a bunch of sophistic bunk that is! North Vietnamese, South Vietnamese, American, what does it matter? Flesh is flesh. And it is indivisible. I am of one body with the tortured (and the torturer?). It is my flesh that is being violated.*

MIND: *I'm sorry but the world can't operate on the basis of such poetic and grandiose identifications. Your pretense that all flesh is yours (and I suppose you would go on to make the world your body) is a neurotic, omnipotent fantasy. You want to be God, to be linked to everything that happens. You should pay attention to your responsibility for digesting this evening's dinner and quit trying to digest the world. Terrible things happen in war, but in fact you are not involved in this incident. So cool it!*

This dialogue points clearly to one element of sacred demand at the heart of the carnal. The viscera has a natural sense of the sacred. It knows that flesh ought to be reverenced, that it is inviolable. Thus its "Goddamn" is to be taken literally as the

cry of an outraged sense of the holy. Nor is it the case that
the instinct for self-preservation dictates that each man should
protect only his own flesh. The normal visceral reaction to
carnage is to be nauseated and want to vomit. This constitutes
the deepest possible witness to the reality of universal identification. The viscera is not separated from the imagination,
except by the inhuman decommissioning of the conscience
which national governments undertake to perform in the time
of war. The healthy imagination creates a visceral connection
between the self and other selves. Note, for instance, how the
young mother flinches when her child is given an injection.
The stomach knows that what happens to one happens to all,
even if the mind tries to deny it. Its undigestable outrage is
an index of the ability of the flesh to locate sacrilege.

Thus a categorical imperative issues from the viscera:
"Reverence the flesh of all men as you reverence your own."
This imperative rests upon compassion or dramatic identification with the flesh of another. It is this identification which is
the basis of ethics. Obligation arises out of feeling, the categorical imperative out of compassion (contrary to Kant).
Men with any feeling for the inviolability of their own bodies
would not tolerate the violation of other men's bodies. There
can be no such thing as a compassionate "body count" to establish the losses of the enemy. Where bodies are counted, the
machine-bodies of the living, already dead to passion and compassion, preside over the funeral of other dead bodies. There
are no men present at such a funeral, unless, somehow in spite
of indoctrination, there remain tears for *all* the flesh now dead
to feeling.

Thus far we have suggested that a fully incarnate and
situated individual may discover the sacred in both its succoring
and demanding dimensions by coming into touch with his own
feelings and his immediate experience. Many theologians and
antitheologians will insist, however, that we have not yet
shown the possibility of a carnal *theology*. Theology, they will

say, deals not with the sacred but with God, not with anything that can be identified within the fleeting moment but with something that transcends time. Good humanists will argue that since man is carnal and historical, he can by definition have no knowledge of anything transcending history, and therefore a carnal theology is a contradiction in terms. Theologians will likely argue that God has chosen to reveal himself at the heart of the carnal, but that I have not yet dealt with those crucial events (the Exodus and the Resurrection) in which this revelation has taken place. The question is, therefore, legitimate. Does a fully incarnate view of man allow us to do theology; does it allow us to speak of God, or merely of something sacred which is homogenized into the world of everyday experience? The viscera may lead us as far as pantheism, but can it justify a theistic vision of reality?

In order to think about the possibility and limits of a visceral theology, there are two things we must keep in mind: (1) Man is carnal and thus all *knowledge* is limited to the soil of historical experience. (2) Although man's knowledge is limited to the earth, his *horizon* is not. An ineradicable mystery surrounds each human life and this ultimately unknowable is as important to the definition of man as is the penultimately knowable. The unknown and the known form the figure-ground, the Gestalt, in terms of which human identity is forged out.

No antimetaphysical fiat issued in the name of positivism, operationalism, or scientism can eradicate the perennial human need to position the self in some consistent manner toward the mysterious context of existence. How are we to understand that mystery out of which we come and into which we disappear? There are three fundamental choices which may be made: the ultimate context of human existence is (1) alien and hostile (gnosticism), (2) friendly and careful (the religious option), or (3) neutral (scientism).

We have earlier stated the fundamental principle of an incarnate view of man: as a man is in his body, so will he be in the world. We may now broaden and extrapolate this view and form a second principle which is the basis of a visceral theology: *as a man is in the world, so will he be in the mystery that founds, sustains, and engulfs the known world.* A correlation can be established between a person's attitudes toward (1) his body, (2) his social and material context, and (3) his ultimate context. If I am suspicious of my body and believe that feelings must be severely disciplined, the chances are I will be sympathetic with a social system in which law and order are the highest values, and will also view the ultimate context of human life as governed by law and regularity. The dominant symbols I use to express this commitment may as easily be political (law and order), psychological (strengthen the ego), philosophical (trust in natural law), or theological (God as lawgiver-Logos). If, on the other hand, my dominant conviction is that my body and my feelings can be trusted, the likelihood is that I will adopt a more liberal view of both political and ultimate reality. Novelty rather than law, possibility rather than necessity will be seen as dominant. It is easiest to see the correlation between attitudes about the body, nature, the political order, and the metaphysical order in a historical phenomenon such as gnosticism. Gnosticism consistently saw an alien God (the Demiurge) as the creator of the body, the *polis,* and the cosmos. Thus all were to be equally suspected and rejected by the man in quest of salvation. Whether such neat correlations can always be traced is yet to be tested. (Thus the crying need for empirical investigations of the functional significance of different types of metaphysical and religious contexting symbols.) At any rate, we are only seeking to show that some notion of God may be compatible with an incarnate view of man that affirms that the body is to be trusted. We do not claim that such a notion is necessary. If, however, we wish to use the word "God," it should signify that the mystery that is the ultimate context of human existence is to be trusted in the same manner as the body and the world are to be trusted. A stance of openness, expectancy, and what Erikson called "basic trust" is to be adopted toward all those dimensions of reality that impinge upon the individual but are beyond his ultimate control.

If we remain close to the certainties of earth, our theology will be at a minimum. We may use the word "God" to signify the unity and trustworthiness of the unknowable source and end of all mundane reality but we may not claim to have *knowledge* of God. An honest theology is necessarily agnostic. No human being can occupy a position from which he can legitimately claim knowledge either of the nature of God or of the adequacy of some constellation of historical events or persons to serve as a revelation of God. The word "God" serves an indispensable function for the man who wishes to make a consistent affirmation of the trustworthiness of the mystery which surrounds his existence, but it is not a word to which he may give a content. We may say the idea of God *functions* (as what Kant called a limit concept) to unify our affirmations about the unknown source and end of mundane reality and to make appropriate certain aspirations and ways of acting. It may be that a theology which takes the incarnation of man seriously should return to the ancient Jewish custom of using the name of God but once a year. In this manner we might at once testify to the importance of the idea of God and the aspirations and actions which are involved in commitment to such an idea, and at the same time keep ourselves free of the pretense that we may know God. An honest theologian will recognize that although he knows *why* he must say the word "God," he does not know *what* he means when he says it. He knows the function of the term but not its definition. And it is sufficient justification for using the term if it can be shown that human life is rendered more hopeful, open, and creative when we dare to speak of God than when we do not.

If a visceral theology is inevitably agnostic in its views about

God, it nevertheless may be highly knowledgeable about the sacred. Indeed, we might define the task of theology as an empirical mapping of the variety of the human experiences of the sacred. Theology is, at best, phenomenology. Or, if we may coin a bad word "numenology," the science of the appearance of the sacred in human experience. Its task is the continual exploration of the changing ways in which the graceful and the inviolable appear in human experience. In pursuing this task it is obliged to invade many different disciplines and language games in search of those elements which actually function to render human life more graceful and inviolable. Religion is a concern of theology only to the degree that it fulfills these conditions. In a given age it may be politics, or art, or psychology, or education in which the most lucid testimony to the sacred is to be found. It is the continual task of the theologian to distinguish between the sacred and the rhetoric of the sacred, because the rhetoric of the sacred, whether used in politics (In God We Trust) or in religion (You *must* believe in the Lord Jesus Christ to be saved), may actually function to demean human life.

IV | Some Practical Implications— Toward a Resurrection of the Bodily

The notion of a visceral theology is not likely to be welcomed by religious professionals. If theology has such a modest content (the explanation of the function of the word "God") and if the sacred is to be found in the mundane, is any place left for religious institutions? If the church is no longer the sole guardian of the sacred in its words testifying to the memory of the "once-upon-a-time" incarnation of the sacred in the history of Israel, what has it to offer that justifies its survival?

I do not want, at this point, to go into the question of the necessity for organizations and institutions. Suffice it to say that the contemporary anarchistic-romantic polemic against institutions is naïve, although understandable. I take it that vitality and form, experience and reflection, charisma and organization are always in a dialectical relationship. Therefore the question is not whether we will have organizations and institutions, but what kinds of organizations and institutions. Religious institutions are the inevitable and necessary effort to be responsive to the experience of the sacred. If they have become irrelevant it is not because they are institutions but because they have been unresponsive to the growing edge of the awareness of the sacred. Theology is a dangerous business because it fosters the illusion that there is some necessary connection between talk about God and the experience of the sacred. Any institution which has the audacity to speak in theological language has the obligation to keep its experience close to its rhetoric. Otherwise it may justifiably be labeled hypocritical.

I will state my suggestions for the church in the form of imperatives because I am strongly convinced that institutional fidelity to the experience of the sacred would demand some rather sweeping reforms.

If theology is to be honest to the limits of what is knowable by an incarnate, situated person, it must become far more *humble* than it has been in the past. I am not speaking of the pseudo-humility of a generation of Barthian theologians who shifted the responsibility for the form of Christian theology and institutions to God. Humility means sticking close to the earth, which, translated into psychological and epistemological terms, means close to one's limited, historical, relative experience. A humble theology would be based upon an individual's reflections upon his own experience of the sacred. It would, in effect, be a systematic witness to the sacred as experienced by one existing historical individual. It would seek to be correlated with the experiences of a wider community, but it would not be founded upon any event not democratically available in the present age. Humility in theology means discovering the sacred on native soil.

A visceral theology majors in the sense of *touch* rather than in the sense of *hearing*. That our age is post-Reformation means that it no longer hears the word of God with the ear of faith. The sacred must be rediscovered in what moves and touches us, in what makes us tremble, in what is proximate rather than remote, ordinary rather than extraordinary, native rather than imported.

A visceral theology therefore demands reawakening of the body, the resurrection of the bodily. In Norman Brown's book *Love's Body,* we have a beautiful exposition of what it might mean to do away with repression and return to what Freud called the "polymorphously perverse body of childhood." But Norman Brown makes the one fatal mistake that is so typically Protestant. When he comes to a discussion of the most appropriate expression of the Dionysian or erotic consciousness, he finds it in the word-play which is the essence of poetry. Without denying the urgent need for a more playful use of language, particularly theological language, we must insist that words alone, even poetic words, are not enough. It is the real, literal, carnal body which must be resensitized and educated in the sacredness which lies hidden in its feelings. Talk, gab, words (even words about "the psychosomatic unity of man" or a visceral theology) are impotent to cure us in an age of propaganda.

If there is a connection between the carnal and the sacred, as we have maintained, then the church must become involved in the exploration of ways to reawaken a reverence for the body and its rhythms. There are several obvious places where we might begin. Eastern spirituality has refined physical disciplines of yoga for over two thousand years. Perhaps the time has come when we should ask for some missionaries *from* the East! In the last few years, sensitivity training and encounter groups have helped large numbers to recover their senses. The Sunday morning barrier against being touched or moved (except by the *words* addressed to the congregation-audience) should be torn down. A church composed of a nexus of encounter groups where feelings of anger, trust, and celebration could be shared would have a far greater graceful potential than the currently word-oriented church. It may be time for this generation of clergy to undertake a pilgrimage to Esalen.

The time is ripe to return to the primitive, the primal, the carnal. To repeat Arthur Darby Nock, "Primitive religion is not believed. It is danced." Words, concepts, doctrines, ideas are all very necessary for clarity and for consistent action. There is a time for words. It has lasted from the Reformation to the present. Now we are sick of being inundated in an ocean of verbiage. The word must be rediscovered in the flesh. Religion must return to dance. Perhaps Zorba is the saint for our time.

If the church fails to develop a visceral theology and fails to help modern man rediscover and reverence his flesh and his feelings, it will neglect a source of common grace as well as the seed from which compassion grows. It will thereby turn its back on the incarnation of the sacred in our history, in our flesh.